Ferdinand Lecomte

The War in the United States

Report to the Swiss Military Department

Ferdinand Lecomte

The War in the United States
Report to the Swiss Military Department

ISBN/EAN: 9783337009144

Printed in Europe, USA, Canada, Australia, Japan

Cover: Foto ©ninafisch / pixelio.de

More available books at **www.hansebooks.com**

THE WAR

IN THE

UNITED STATES.

REPORT

TO THE

SWISS MILITARY DEPARTMENT; PRECEDED BY A DISCOURSE
TO THE FEDERAL MILITARY SOCIETY ASSEMBLED
AT BERNE, AUG. 18, 1862.

BY

FERDINAND LECOMTE,
LIEUTENANT-COLONEL, SWISS CONFEDERATION:

Author of "*Relation Historique et Critique de la Campagne d'Italie en 1859;*" "*L'Italie en 1860;*"
and "*Le Général Jomini, sa Vie et ses Ecrits.*"

TRANSLATED FROM THE FRENCH.

NEW YORK:
D. VAN NOSTRAND, 192 BROADWAY.
1863.

Entered according to Act of Congress, in the year 1863, by

D. VAN NOSTRAND,

In the Clerk's Office of the District Court of the United States for the Southern District of New York.

C. A. ALVORD, STEREOTYPER AND PRINTER.

DISCOURSE

ADDRESSED TO THE

FEDERAL MILITARY SOCIETY,

Assembled in Annual Session at Berne, August 18, 1862.

GENTLEMEN OFFICERS:

About two months since, I was requested by our committee to say something at this meeting, of the war in North America, in which I have had the honor of taking a feeble part. I have with pleasure responded to this appeal, in the first place, because it could not be a matter of indifference to republicans that I should speak to them of the misfortunes of another republic; and in the second, because I was gratified to have this opportunity of rectifying some errors which have been current in Europe, in regard to these transactions.

Before speaking, or rather, before speaking to you of the American war, I ought to establish the causes of it. In so doing, I shall be obliged to enter a little upon the domain of politics. It is nothing surprising that in a country so vast as the United States, extending over twenty-five degrees of latitude, comprising, therefore, very different climates, and by consequence different manners,—reckoning thirty-one millions of souls, thirty-four sovereign States, and nine territories, all accustomed to democratic rule,—it is nothing surprising, I say, that in such a country, a great number of parties should exist. Ever since its origin, the struggles of parties there have been incessant and active; but the sentiment of respect for law had always triumphed over the malignity of these contests. Recently, however, this has not been the case.

Three principal parties had succeeded in establishing themselves. One was that of the Southern population, inhabiting a fertile soil, enriching themselves from the products of this soil, particularly from cotton, and employing in its culture African laborers, brought by force to this country and reduced to the condition of slaves. This party is styled *Democratic*, although it would be better named *Oligarchic*. Its social state resembles a little that of the old feudal lords, or the patriarchs of the East. By its homogeneousness, as opposed to the multiple interests of the North, it has almost always succeeded in carrying the candidates of its choice, in the elections for the Presidency.

In opposition to this party of the South, or Slave party, is found one called the Northern, or Republican party, which I shall define, briefly, by saying that it is almost the contrary of that of the South.

Between the two is a mixed party, preferring above every thing else, the enjoyment of the benefits of the Union, and making, for this object, concessions on both hands.

At the last Presidential election, there were four candidates in the field; the ballot was very full and regular; Mr. Lincoln, the candidate of the Republican party, was elected. The Southern States then carried into actual effect the threat which they had long made; and with South Carolina at the head, declared for a separation from the Union. They seized its arsenals, its forts, its custom-houses, its posts; blockaded its garrisons; and finally bombarded the Federal garrison of Fort Sumter, the first act of hostility of the actual campaign.

It became necessary for the Union also to take arms, to re-establish the authority of the Constitution and the laws. Unfortunately, if the Union is well organized to cause the arts of peace to flourish, it has the worst possible adaptation for the direction of war. There is wanting to it the very first instrument of a government, an army. It lacks, besides, unity of command and strength of government. There is a superabundance of criticism, and of political wheel-work, which complicate the progress of military affairs. It is nothing surprising that the first demonstrations of the North had been marked by reverses; and had ended in the defeat of Bull Run, on the 21st of July, 1861. But the North persisted; gave a better organization to its forces; levied five hundred thousand men; and in this second campaign obtained great successes. It might almost have been believed, last June, that the war would terminate,—the great war, I mean,— before Richmond; when new reverses, on the Chickahominy, and in the Shenandoah, caused the Federals to replace themselves on the defensive, and begin another campaign with new levies.

The war therefore will continue, for the Union persists more than ever in wishing to re-establish the unity of its territory; and, besides, peace, in the actual condition of things, would be only a truce of some years, wholly for the advantage of the South. The war will therefore be pursued; and I permit myself to express publicly here my lively and sincere wishes for the final triumph of the North.

I express these wishes, because secession is an *illegality:* it is contrary to the letter and the spirit of the Federal Constitution, to the spirit of every Constitution, and of every organization of political society whatever. If it is allowed to one of the parties to a contract sanctioned by all, to withdraw himself from it without the consent of the others; if it is allowed to South Carolina to separate herself from the old Union, how can the right be refused to Virginia, for example, to separate herself from the new? How can the right be refused to a county, or subordinate division (commune), to separate itself from the State; to a family to withdraw itself from the county; to an individual to liberate himself from society, and to arm himself against it? This doctrine of secession leads straight to anarchy, and is only, at bottom, a subtle theory of the right of force and of barbarism.

I express also my wishes for the Union, because secession is an *injustice*, and an iniquitous act. Let it be granted that the inhabitants of a country may quit it *en masse;* it may be admitted that they have a right to do so, and that in so doing they injure chiefly themselves. But that they should carry away the territory, which is a property of the State, is another thing. The frontiers would be changed, as well as the conditions of prosperity and security to those who remain. The Union is an entirety, an edifice which has been in course of erection for a long period, and not a heap of pebble stones thrown pell-mell the one beside the other. If one of the fractions of this edifice, if a single panel of the wall, is withdrawn, it is not only the removal of that panel, which is produced, but the falling in of the whole.

In the particular case, it is to strip the Union of advantages which it has acquired at the price of heavy sacrifices. It is the Union which has aggrandized the South, and led her to a height of riches and power which cause her to think to-day of her separation. It was the Union which purchased Louisiana for sixty millions of francs from the Emperor Napoleon; it was the Union, and not the South, which purchased Florida; which has procured the annexation of Texas; which made war against Mexico, against the English, and has several times come near getting into a war with Spain,—having been thrown into these troubles chiefly by, and for the advantage of, the Southern States. If the Union has made these sacrifices, it is, in part, in order to have possession of the outlet of her great artery of navigation in the west, the Mississippi, which she cannot leave in hostile hands; it is to open for herself an access to the Gulf of Mexico; to have the anchorages necessary for her marine upon the Atlantic: and she has succeeded, in fact, in becoming a great maritime nation. To take from her three-fourths of her coasts, as the South wishes to do, and the outlets of her great basins, is entirely to change her situation, and to strip her of that which constitutes her strength. It is, in a word, to strike a death-blow at the Union.

Does any great idea, any supreme interest of humanity, any political principle, at least, religious or national, inflame the Southern mind in its culpable enterprise? Alas, no! It is not for the assertion of the rights of a particular nationality, since all the inhabitants of the South as well as of the North, are, in large majority, of the same Anglo-Saxon race, and speak the same English tongue. Nor is it undertaken in the name of a religious principle, as was the thirty years' war. Not only are the people all Christians, but the great mass at the South, as well as the North, belongs to the same Protestant confession, to the same church system, to independent churches, free from all connection with the State. Political divergences are not more sensible. All are democratic; the constitutions of the different States, North and South, are almost identical; a legislative power of two chambers, a governor as the executive power, universal suffrage, the liberty of the press, the right of association, etc., are common features of all these constitutions.

In spite of all that, it should be avowed that there is an idea in this raising of the shield of the South, but a detestable idea. Slavery, which she believes to be in danger (and she is right), has put arms in her hands. It is for the defence, it is for the great glory of this abominable institution, which shames the civilization and the Christian sentiments of our age, that she has put herself at war with her brethren.

It is pretended in Europe, I am aware, that slavery is not at stake in this war. Nothing equals the falsity of this assertion, except its effrontery. It is besides enhanced by a certain malice, which demands some examination.

No! slavery is not at issue in this war, if it is thought that the North has undertaken a sanguinary crusade against the South to bring about the immediate emancipation of all the blacks, without giving herself any uneasiness about the difficulties in the way, and about certain economic necessities. Without doubt there is a party in the North, a party ardent, vigorous, and embracing a great number of men of talent and of faith, which would be inclined to proceed in this manner, because it thinks that slavery is at the same time an evil so great, and a crime so horrible, that no consideration tending to retard its suppression, can be put in comparison with it. But this party, if it is, perhaps, the very nucleus of the great Northern party, is not its head, and if its ideas are generally admitted in principle, its means of execution are reprobated.

By the side of this party is found another, or rather another shade of party, which is composed of men not less convinced, but more practical, more careful of the consequences of their acts, and, besides, placed under a heavy responsibility, since its principal members are of the government. This party can be judged by its acts, which are official decisions. It is seen by these that this party too desires the suppression of slavery, but that it desires to proceed towards the end more calmly, and more surely than the abolitionists. It wishes to adhere to the law, as far as possible, and to avoid revolutionary and violent measures. Thus it has given the example, within the limits of its power, and decreed the enfranchisement of the slaves within the Federal District of Columbia, with indemnity to the proprietors. This the South always opposed.

The Federal Government has also decided, using a right recognized for every belligerent, to confiscate the slaves of its adversaries in arms, and to liberate them; all the fugitive blacks which have been employed in the war, are also declared free. It is readily seen that the war will result, by this single means, in the liberation of a great number of slaves. I may observe further, that there are already forty thousand in this condition. The Congress of Washington has followed by proclaiming emancipation as an object of public utility; and the resources of the Union will be pledged to all the States which may wish to rid themselves of this plague. Severe measures have been taken against the trade in contrabands, and, finally, a slave-trader has been executed in New York, which, in view of the rareness of the fact, has produced a great and salutary sensation. In fine, the Northern party has shown that it did not wish only the emancipation of the slave, but also the rehabilitation of the negro race, still, from a condescension to the Southern spirit, too much despised even in the North. The liberated blacks will receive territories which they will colonize, and which they will be able, one day, to have admitted into the Union by the same title as the others. The black republics of Hayti and Liberia have been recognized, to which the South was always opposed; and, henceforth, black ambassadors will be reckoned in the diplomatic corps at Washington.

It is seen, therefore, that on the side of the North, slavery is a decided interest in the war; and whether it be continued, or whether the government of Mr. Lincoln shall soon enter upon the full exercise of its authority, the solution of this great problem will be positively advanced. In this it is by no means intended to say that the Federal Government intends to place itself in opposition to legal rights, and to the Constitution, which it represents.

But if we direct our attention particularly to the South, we see that slavery is its great motive to the war. The people of the South do not wish to hear a word spoken of abolition, either gradual or immediate. They wish, on the contrary, to cause to be recognized their right to extend slavery into all the territories, and to cause this right to be protected. Slavery has become, for these populations, not only a fact, useful or injurious according to the several points of view, but a doctrine which has penetrated all institutions, a dogma which, according to them, ought to command the respect of the entire world. Their constitution determines the consequences of slavery; their discourses, their proclamations, their conversations, their threats, their complaints, their history, and especially the recent troubles of Kansas, all testify that it is slavery—its prosperity, its extension, the fear of its diminution,—which has thrown the South into the war. Their priests even preach the sanctity of it. And for every man not prejudiced, it remains certain, that if the South has refused to recognize the act of the majority of the nation of which it has formed a constituent part; if it has brutally torn the Constitution, to whose observance it has sworn; if it desires the destruction of the Union which has afforded it protection, and of a country of which the prodigious increase and prosperity have demonstrated the importance in the world;—if the South wishes to commit this double crime, it is that she may the more readily commit one greater still,—that of the maintenance and extension of slavery.

This being so, how happens it that Europe, which prides itself on being humane and Christian, receives with so much bitterness every thing which is favorable to the North in this crisis, and seems to devote all its sympathies to the South? It is for a very simple reason. Let me be permitted to say it frankly, without being accused of going in quest of sounding words: it is because Europe, covered for the most part with oligarchic and despotic institutions, hates democracies in general, and the great American Republic in particular.

We Swiss, although we may be but a small State, although we may believe ourselves weak, and that we should willingly respect our obligations of European neutrality, which are in other respects such as are agreeable to us, already know something of this matter.

But the union of the United States occasions greater umbrage. It is, or rather it was, a great democracy, rich, prosperous, improvising on the instant armies of a million of men; possessing a military marine which at this time, thanks to its improve ments, is the first of the world; proclaiming its political liberties to all; preaching them by her example; not recognizing any slavish obligation of neutrality, and putting herself in alliance or in war with whomsoever it may seem good to her, without rendering any account of her conduct to any one. This country gives offence because she is not only strong, but every day a little less removed from Europe. Fifty years ago the passage was reckoned in months; twenty years ago it was counted only by weeks; to-day it is by days,—ten days. In twenty years, without doubt, it will be less still. And then it is a-disagreeable country as a neighbor; blacksmiths there become Presidents of the republic; printers' laborers become ministers; carpenters and boys of the coffee-house, become senators and generals, and good generals too. The poor fugitive, embarked from Europe with his wallet and love of liberty as his whole fortune, finds there a sure asylum—more than an asylum; a country which gives him a good reception if he is honest and courageous; which facilitates his labors in the interior; which protects him at a dis. tance, as at Smyrna, against arbitrary power; which enriches him if he is active and enterprising; which raises him in consideration, and even sends him back to Europe, who drove him from her, as the Ambassador of a great people. Ah! yes, it is perhaps disagreeable for some persons in Europe to see their ports approach such a nation, which not only represents an opposite principle, but presents herself sometimes as a living reproach. And then, say they, these Americans are so rude, so abrupt, haughty, boastful, impertinent, insolent, egotistic, thinking only of making money. It is true that it is added also to these griefs, that they speak through the nose; that they chew their tobacco with their mouths full; that they spit on the boots of their neighbor; that they place their feet upon the table, and that they forget often to take out the handkerchief to blow the nose. But if they have not, as the ancient aristocracy of our Europe, the monopoly of all the graces, they have, on the other hand, solid qualities.

They are free of heart; they are firm of character; they are good parents; they are proud citizens; they have a consciousness of their republican dignity; they are pious; they are laborious; and to them it belongs more than to any others to say, with our beautiful national song: "We have no master but God."*

Then, besides, they are inventive, ingenious, they have a fever for business, a passion for progress; they have covered their soil with canals, with railroads and telegraphs, reaping a harvest for the United States as do the ordinary roads for Europe. They have

* Excepté Dieu, nous n'avons point de maîtres.

pushed the boldness of their marine to the limits of the impossible; they have opened immense territories to colonization; snatched from the earth its most hidden mineral treasures, and spanned the arms of the sea by gigantic bridges. They follow and outstrip everywhere, the English in their commercial explorations; they have created a thousand sources of prosperity for individuals, all the while advancing the arts of civilization and the reign of Christianity. They had demonstrated the possibility of a great democracy, the creative power of liberty, whatever an august voice may have said, which pretended, not long ago, that liberty was good only to serve as an ornament to an edifice founded without it.

This was enough to draw upon her the rancor of despotic and oligarchic Europe. She has, however, herself not been at fault. For fifty years these blows have been falling upon the United States, and they are attacked to-day with more fury than ever.

With what were they reproached not long since? It was particularly with habits of lawlessness and of turbulence; the troubles of Kansas; the licentious band of fillibusters against Mexico, against Cuba, &c.

And to-day, when the Union, beholding the rise of a monstrous violation of law, sets herself, as in duty bound, to re-establish the authority of the national law, Europe takes part for the rebels! Rebellion, which is a crime on this side of the ocean, in Hungary, in Venice, in the Ionian Isles, in the streets of Paris, in the East Indies, and that under governments which do not boast of their clemency, becomes a right in the West Indies, a holy thing against the government of the United States, which asks only of those subject to her authority to refrain from pillaging her posts, her custom-houses, and her arsenals! Strange contradiction, which is, however, not the greatest.

With the shameful plague of slavery, the immense success obtained by "Uncle Tom's Cabin" was brought to mind; the ovations to its author; then the complaints of the English against the American traders in contraband; the reproaches addressed to the United States in 1854, because they chose to remain absolute neutrals between the allies and Russia. It was well worthy of the slave republic, said they, to ally herself with the Muscovite empire and her serfs. Russia, under the impulse of her liberal emperor of the day, proceeds boldly to the establishment of equality, and Europe applauds the act. The United States do the same; they do more; they are thrown into a war which should decide the future of slavery, and Europe turns upon them her back, to avow her sympathies for the States of the South.

She pretends that her interest imposes upon her this policy. What! a great country suffers from a crisis whose effects are recognized to extend also to Europe: the question is to know, not only whether cotton shall be more or less abundant, but whether four millions of human beings who produce it, shall be condemned to a degradation as durable as their descendants, and Europe, an accomplice in these struggles by her abolition agitations, should concern herself with the consequences, only in so far as regards the cotton ports and her manufactures! In opposition to the cross of the Gospel, which the North places upon her banner, it is Europe which would elevate the golden calf! I refuse to believe it.

I do not wish to examine, in order not to abuse your attention, what are the pretended interests, so superior, which are invoked here, and which come so seasonably to support the political rancor which I have indicated; for when I see before me great principles of Christian equality applying themselves to four millions of men in one scale of the balance, I have no idea of any mercantile interest whatever, daring to place itself in the other.*

---

* Lieutenant-Colonel Le Comte then reads some fragments of his report to the Military Department, and the assembly, on the proposition of M. the Federal Colonel Kurz, decide to have it published. It is to respond to this desire that the "Swiss Military Review" commences to-day the present publication.

REPORT

TO THE

SWISS MILITARY DEPARTMENT.

M. THE FEDERAL COUNSELLOR:

Returned happily to Switzerland from the campaign which you had authorized me to make in the United States of America, by your honored letter of the 11th December, 1861, I have the honor of submitting to you the following report:

I ought to state in the first place, that, thanks to my quality of a Swiss federal officer, and to the recommendations of the Federal Military Department; to those of General Dufour; of M. Fogg, Ambassador of the United States at Berne; and of some other persons, I was very well received by Mr. Seward, Secretary of State, by Mr. Stanton, Secretary of War, by General McClellan, at that time commanding in chief all the Federal forces, as also by our consuls at New York and Washington, De Luze and Hitz.

General McClellan, whose head-quarters were then

at Washington, deigned to attach me to his staff as voluntary aide-de-camp, retaining my Swiss rank of Major, and with the condition of being able to return at any time to my country, should I be called thither by my government. I met, on the staff of General McClellan, with several European officers, who were held in that position with the same title as myself.

I have already had the honor, M. Federal Counsellor, of presenting to you at Berne the letters of leave which were delivered to me by General McClellan and by the Secretary of War.

I.

THEATRE OF WAR.—GENERAL STATISTICAL AND GEOGRAPHICAL NOTIONS.

For the understanding of the observations which I desire to present under this head, it is necessary that I recall briefly some of the principal features of the country.

The United States of America, the theatre of the existing civil war, constitute a vast federative republic, of thirty-four States and nine Territories. Bounded on the north by the British Possessions; on the west by the Pacific Ocean; on the south by the republic and the Gulf of Mexico; and on the east by the Atlantic Ocean,—she comprises an extent of three millions two hundred and fifty thousand square miles, that is to say, an area almost equal to that of all Europe.

In respect to its physical structure, the country comprises five great regions:

1st. The basin of the Atlantic, extending the whole length of the coast of this sea,—a low plain, reckoning a great number of water-courses;

2d. The region of the Alleghanies, an undulating table-land of fifty leagues in width, on the average, and of small elevation;

3d. The immense basin of the Mississippi and its affluents, comprising therein the prairies of the West;

4th. The chains and the plateaus of the Rocky Mountains,—an arid and almost desert country;

5th. The Pacific basin, at the extreme west of the continent.

It is in the basins of the Mississippi and of the Atlantic, that are found the two principal theatres of the present war.

It is not useless to remark that these five divisions extend from north to south, over the whole territory of the United States, between 25° and 29' of latitude, without any great transverse intersection occurring to divide the country geographically into North and South.

The total population of the United States is about thirty-one millions and a half of inhabitants, of which nearly four millions are black slaves, and four hundred thousand red skin Indians. The census of 1860 proves, during the last ten years, an increase of population of about eight million souls, of which nearly one million are blacks.

The immense majority of the inhabitants of the North and of the South are of the same race—the Anglo-Saxon; of the same language—the English; and of the same religion—the Protestant.

The ways of communication are numerous in the inhabited countries. The great development of the coasts, and of the navigable interior waters, the canals, the railroads, present vast means of circulation. The soil of the North and of the Northwest of the United States, is interlaced with iron ways; and it may be said that there are as many of them as of ordinary roads, in many parts of Europe far advanced in government.

One may convince himself of this by the subjoined table of railroads in 1862.* I should not pretend to present an exact statement, which would not have possessed great importance in a military point of view, since one may go almost everywhere by railway,—having myself been already conveyed over ten thousand leagues of this kind of road, distributed amongst more than seventy companies.

There are ten grand arteries connecting the Atlantic with the Mississippi, and as many descending from the Lakes towards the Gulf of Mexico and the Atlan-

* Not printed.

tic. A short time hence, a railroad will connect the Mississippi with the Pacific, across the Rocky Mountains.

The principal centres of the networks, or rather of the skeins, of railroad are: the cities of New York, Boston, Philadelphia, Baltimore, Richmond, Cincinnati, St. Louis, Louisville, Nashville, Indianapolis, Milwaukie, Chicago, Buffalo, Cleveland, &c. The principal gaps are observed to be in the South.

On the other hand, at the South, as well as the North, ordinary routes and neighborhood roads are rather rare than abundant.

The parties to the struggle are, on the one side, the regular and lawful government of the Union, supported by twenty-one States of the North; and on the other, a certain number of States, all of the South, and all slave States, which have successively increased to the number of eleven, and joined in one Confederacy.

The different denominations in vogue for the distinction of the parties in the strife, are, on the one hand:

The States of the North—Unionists, Federals, Loyals, Free State men, Republicans, Yankees.

And on the other side:

States of the South—Slave States, Confederates, Secessionists, Separatists, Rebels.

The first are:

California, Connecticut, Delaware, Illinois, Indiana,

Iowa, Kansas, Maine, Maryland, Massachusetts, Michigan, Minnesota, New Hampshire, New Jersey, New York, Ohio, Oregon, Pennsylvania, Rhode Island, Vermont, Wisconsin.

Total, twenty-one States; of which two only (Delaware and Maryland) are slave States.

The secession, or rebel States, according to the appellation of the North, which refuses them the name of belligerents, are:

Alabama, Arkansas, North Carolina, South Carolina, Florida, Georgia, Louisiana, Mississippi, Tennessee, Texas, Virginia.

Total, eleven States,—all slave States.

Kentucky, a slave State, solicited by two parties of almost equal strength, sought to remain neutral, and was tossed about according to the caprices of the fortune of arms. It is at present in the hands of the Federals. Missouri and Virginia parcelled themselves out. The Federal District of Columbia remained to the Government of the Union; and the territories of the West, without taking a determinate position, were rather with the Union than against her.

The population of the twenty-one Northern States is about twenty-one millions of souls, of which nearly a million are slaves, for the most part in Maryland. That of the Southern States rises to ten millions of souls, of which more than three and a half millions are slaves.

II.

CAUSES OF THE WAR.

It is not easy to give in a few lines, as I must limit myself to do here, a just and complete idea of the causes of the war.

To do this, it would be necessary to go back to the very origin of the nation, to the British colonies, and to follow their development down to our days, through the struggles for independence and the era of the foundation of the republic.

It may be said, in a general way, that the antagonism of the South and the North, which has produced the present hostilities, had its first origin in the great difference of climate of a country extending over 25° of latitude,—a difference developing in its turn, according to the principles already recognized by Montesquieu, very different manners and institutions.

The causes of the war existed already in embryo in the first acts of the colonists who founded the great Republic. The oppositions of climate caused them to blossom and grow.

These first colonists introduced, on the one side, slavery of the blacks as a domestic institution legally guaranteed; and, on the other side, the Christian enthusiasm, the ardent faith, of the English Puritans of the seventeenth century, flying from Europe through love of their convictions.

At first, slavery prevailed in all the British colonies, as well as in the adjacent territories of the South. But under the influence of favorable geographical circumstances, it developed itself especially in the South, where the blacks are employed in the culture of products of the torrid zone, viz.: sugar, cotton, indigo, rice, and tobacco.

The usefulness of the blacks; their material well-being, sufficiently general, in comparison with the lot of the low class of European populations; the moral and intellectual progress of their situation over that which they would have had in their native country, still devoted to idolatry and to barbarism,—including therein slavery ; by slow degrees brought the planters of the South to an accommodation with the Christian dogmas of human equality. " If God," say they, " had wished that our African laborers should be our equals, He would not have made them black ; they bear, in their color, and ought to bear in their inferior social position, the weight of the sin of their first father, the accursed Ham."

Under the shield of this surrender of conscience, slavery prospered in the South of the United States, becoming there not only a useful agricultural agent, but an important branch of commerce, and of industry. The rearing of the blacks, the traffic in them, and their sale occupied more persons every year. This entirely special *article* of merchandise, which could be diminished or increased from itself, demanded special protections. Soon the laws and the codes manifested a preference for it, and slavery of the blacks, as a fact and as a doctrine, pervaded every institution. It came to form the basis of domestic society, at the same time that it became more and more, by the contests of parties, the motive and the object of all political action. From the moment that it appeared menaced by its adversaries, it was surrounded with preservatives of every kind; and the more it was attacked from without, the more dear it became within. From a simple agricultural fact, more or less injurious, which it was at its origin, it is to-day exalted in the South, to the height of a dogma, at the same time political, religious, economical, which ought to command the respect of the whole world, and, above all, that of the members of the common republic.

In the North, on the contrary, the black was not found in favorable climatic conditions.

Agriculture did not there require the rude labors, and did not yield the rich products of that of the South; manufactures, which there supplied its place, did not afford advantageous employment to African laborers. It was found more profitable, and probably also more Christian, to get rid of them; some were emancipated, others were sold to the South.

Besides, it is at the North that the great flood of European emigration discharges itself. The poor Irish, traditionally devoted to domestic life; the patient Germans; all nations enterprising and robust, came and mingled among the blacks, without thinking that they kept up the current of religious principles, opposed to the brutal servitude of one race to another.

Under this triple influence, slavery gradually retired from the North; then it was banished from points where some accidental circumstances might have been able to fasten it; then, at last, it was shamed as a detestable institution.

The great powers of Europe, which adopted a like course of action for their colonies, contributed to fortify the sentiments of the *Abolitionists* of America. There were soon but two slave States north of the Potomac, and there are but two now,—Maryland and Delaware, and still each year the blacks diminish there.

For a sufficiently long time the struggle between these two opppsite tendencies of the North and South, rested in the domain of philosophy and religion. The churches and the philanthropic societies of Boston, and of New York, preached human equality to those of Richmond and Charleston, which replied by sermons on the spirit of envy, jealousy, and political oppression.

The States being themselves sovereign within the limits of the Federal Constitution, which guaranteed the property of all, it was necessary that some time should pass by before this struggle should transfer itself to the domain of national politics; and the antagonism between the defenders and the adversaries of slavery appeared in the Federal elections, only as a reserved plan, and subordinate to other divisions of parties.

But two orders of facts, chiefly, came by small degrees, to enlarge the field of this question.

There were, in the first place, contests to which fugitive slaves gave rise, the extradition of whom by one State to another, is imposed as a duty in the Federal Constitution itself. It is a fact that many persons of the North used their best endeavors to thwart the reclamations of the proprietors of slaves; and that, in place of aiding in the restoration of the *fugitives*, they have often used all their efforts to protect their flight. It resulted from this state of things, that frequent difficulties developed themselves before the tribunals of the States or of the Union, and the judgments of these converted the local question of slavery into one of Federal concern.

Matters went farther. The South made lively complaint of the insufficiency of the constitutional provisions to prevent the escape of their property, and, in 1850, it obtained from Congress, by an adroit manœuvre of a coalition of parties, a Draconian law. on the escape and the recovery of slaves. This inhuman law remained, for the most part, a dead letter in several States of the North. They did not deny its authority, as South Carolina had before done the law of the tariff, but its execution was paralyzed, and its provisions eluded a hundred times. The subject matter of dispute was wonderfully favorable to that course of treatment, and, ordinarily, the reclaimed slave succeeded in proving that he was the victim of a bargain, or in escaping further off. Thus, with the view of strengthening or weakening the execution of this law, the parties which took their position on the question of slavery were naturally led to take a more important part in the different Federal and State elections.

The other order of facts, was the creation of new Territories, and their admission as States into the Union.

Should slavery be protected there, or not?

The North pretended generally that slavery ought not to be extended, and supported herself by the example of the founders of the Republic, who had refused to sanction it in the only Territory of that time. The South sustained the opposite proposition, relying also upon the authority of the founders of the Republic, who had guaranteed the equality of rights and of property in the Constitution itself, comprising therein that of slaves.

In this respect a double struggle ordinarily takes place; first, in the Territory itself,—especially when located near the two sections,—whether its constitution shall or shall not protect slavery; and then in the Union, whether the new State shall be admitted or rejected, according as it is with or without slaves.

The admission of Louisiana in 1812, previously purchased of France, was the occasion of lively complaints on the part of the North. This State was nevertheless admitted with its slave constitution.

The same dispute recurred eight years later, on the occasion of the admission of Missouri. The North still yielded to a compromise, called the Missouri Compromise, which forever excluded slavery from the Territories situated north of a line passing by the northern frontier of Missouri—that is to say, by 36° and 30′ of latitude. This decision was equivalent, for the South, to a guarantee of slavery in all the Territories of its own neighborhood, which it hoped to colonize, or one day to acquire, and was considered by it a great triumph.

The admission of Arkansas as a slave State in 1836; that of Florida in 1845, which had also been purchased by the Union in 1819; then that of Texas, detached from Mexico; then, finally, the prospective riches which were opened up by the victorious war against Mexico, and the peace which was imposed on it in 1847—were new successes for the South, which saw approaching the moment when it should rule in Congress.

But, on the other hand, movements for colonization on the part of the North were accelerated by the construction of railways, and by the discovery of the auriferous treasures of California. This Territory, detached from Mexico, entered the Union in 1850 as a State, without slaves. Some years before, the States of Michigan, Iowa, Wisconsin, and Minnesota had been admitted by the same title, without reckoning other territories in these countries offering to the North an easy colonization.

Two other Territories, situated on the limits of the Missouri Compromise, were likely to render the situation more difficult. These were Kansas and Nebraska, colonized at first by the Missourians, who peopled Kansas with sufficient rapidity, and who reckoned on easily making the neighboring States slave States.

But in order to do that, it was necessary first to overcome the Missouri Compromise, and the barrier of 36° 30′ of latitude.

After very active controversies, and parliamentary struggles, the South obtained this concession also from Congress, by a coalition of sordid interests. The Union in 1850 abandoned its power over the question of slavery, in favor of the Territories themselves. These were declared open to colonization by both sections, and free to adapt the question of slavery to their own circumstances and convenience. The people of the North did not admit themselves beaten. They organized and excited the emigration of their people to Kansas; struggled with persistence against the invasion of the Missourians; opposed, on the occasion, force to force, and, after a period of agitation and of violence, they succeeded at last in obtaining the majority. Kansas prepared a Constitution proscribing slavery, under which she demanded her admission into the Union.

Great was the rage of the South, which then already threatened a resort to arms, and which succeeded by magnifying the incidents in connection with Kansas in causing the postponement of the admission of the new State. It was admitted only in January, 1861—that is to say, after the secession had taken place.

Nebraska remained still, as a Territory, an open arena; but the South has succeeded in transporting thither only thirty slaves, at most.

At the same time, in 1859, Oregon was a new recruit for the North.

Another cause of the war, having relation to the same geographical circumstances which have produced that of slavery, is the difference of social activity; of the means of acquiring riches; and, by consequence, of the material interests actually existing between the North and the South.

The first is principally manufacturing and commercial; the second is chiefly agricultural. The latter grows rich while furnishing its products,—its cotton among others,—to Europe, which has need of them; the former takes charge of the exportation of those products.

The States of the South are, besides, a market for the manufacturers of the North, and the latter is very glad to exclude from it foreign competition. Hence her predilection for a system of tariffs, which aid her in struggling against English industry, but of which the South, as consumer, pretends herself the principal victim.

The theories and their definitions thus clashing, the North and the South are seen to divide, in respect to commerce, into "protectionists" and "free traders." By a strange and ridiculous mode of expression, the South, all whose institutions look towards the protection of its special and only object of industry, slavery, and all whose efforts have reference to obtaining for it the protection of the Union, calls itself free trade! But the partisans of tariffs have a long time had the majority in Congress, not only on account of the principle itself, but also because the customs have the advantage of returning large revenues to the state, which, without them, it would be necessary to supply otherwise. It is the South, besides, which was one of the introducers of tariffs in 1816, after the war against the English; and she has discovered that, in so doing, she has served the North more than herself. An attempt made in 1840 to reduce the tariff led to an industrial crisis, which ceased only by a return to protection in 1842. Since then it has been increased still more.

In this same order of ideas, the marine and the tonnage of the United States have been protected against foreign competition by a law styled a naviga tion law, or rather a tonnage law, which has the appearance of increasing the cost of transportation, and of raising the price of commodities for exportation. The South, careful, above all, in regard to its cotton, —King Cotton, as they call it,—complains bitterly of this law, although it may be proven that spite of this pretended restraint, the South cannot even furnish cotton enough to satisfy the demand.

Under these three aspects: danger to its slave property, which cannot prosper to a degree which would satisfy her ambition; protective tariffs; encouragement to the coastwise trade,—the South pretends herself duped and practised upon by the North. The familiar mode of expressing her complaints is to style herself, the *milch cow* of the North.

As a compensation, and as a guarantee, the South wishes at least to have the possession of the principal positions in the Federal government. If she did not succeed in obtaining the complete triumph of her views and her interests, she permitted herself to reckon on some moderation in the execution of measures to her disadvantage; while, at the same time, obtaining for herself certain lucrative employments and positions. It seems, indeed, that the North, tired of the strife, had for a long time acquiesced in these pretensions, by a kind of tacit agreement, and that it had not attached great importance to having the Federal government in its hands.

It was during these transactions, and under other

influences besides, that the providential election of 1860 took place.

The various political fractions of the North, which hitherto had almost always allowed themselves to separate, came, by reaction against the audacity of the slave pretensions of the South, to unite in a great Republican party, which formed itself definitely at Chicago, and which decided to carry into the Presidency Mr. Abraham Lincoln, of Illinois.

The South divided itself on Mr. Breckinridge, of Kentucky, and Mr. Douglas, a citizen of Illinois, but a slave proprietor in Virginia, and belonging to the Southern or Democratic party. A fourth candidate, a moderate Unionist, Mr. Bell, was put forward to counteract the candidacy of Mr. Lincoln.

An election of unaccustomed excitement followed amongst the people of the States, and in which the South seemed rather to have for her object, to embitter the passions, than to secure the triumph of her candidate. Her part was already taken, to make a rupture, and she persisted in dividing her votes, while at the North the current set in quite an opposite direction.

The sixth of November 1861, Mr. Lincoln was elected by 1,857,610 votes against 1,365,976 cast for Mr. Douglas, 847,953 for Mr. Breckinridge, and 590,631 for Mr. Bell,—a majority which was also confirmed by the electoral vote of the States.

This defeat of the South, which, however, in uniting the votes of the two democratic candidates, found itself in a majority over Mr. Lincoln, was the signal for the tempest.

For a long time already, at each crisis, the orators of the Southern States had threatened a separation, if their wishes should not be complied with. South Carolina, in regard to the tariff law, had even made an attempt in that direction in 1832, but was vigorously repressed by the President, General Jackson. Then, already, the State pretended to the right of nullifying Federal decisions contrary to its interests; and this doctrine, which was anarchic, but skilfully sustained by a man of great talent, Mr. Calhoun, had made sufficiently numerous partisans in the slave States.

Then after the last electoral crisis, many journals and popular orators of the Carolinas, of Virginia, of Georgia, of Lousiana, and of other States besides, had formally declared, that if they *might* consent to submit to the election of Mr. Douglas, or of Mr. Bell, they certainly never could recognize that of Mr. Lincoln as the act of the nation.

It is in fact the very thing, which, contrary to all the principles of law hitherto practically recognized, has actually occurred.

South Carolina, the furnace of the slave party, first put herself forward.

Hardly had the triumph of Mr. Lincoln been announced by the telegraph, before the legislature of that State, sitting at Charleston, decided upon the calling of a national convention* for the 17th of December, which should have to pronounce upon the question of the separation of South Carolina from the Union; or, in other words, on a *secession*. At the same time the greater part of the Federal functionaries of the State or in the State,—at the customs, in the post-offices and at the arsenals, &c.,—resigned their functions, or declared themselves independent. The Virginia senators at Washington quitted their seats.

Georgia, Louisiana, Florida, followed the example of Charleston; and the question of secession, its right, its advantages, its inconveniences became the subject of every discussion. A strong emotion prevailed throughout the South, while the North, confident in her victory, awaited calmly the return of those vanquished by the ballot, to more reasonable sentiments, and the entry of the new President on his duties.

But it was necessary that four months should yet pass by, under the administration of Mr. Buchanan. Of this administration, some of the members by open complicity, others by their weakness alone, allowed, during all this time, the efforts of secession to grow at their pleasure, and assume an organized form.

Treason took part in passing events, and the Minister of War, General Floyd, a proprietor of slaves in Virginia, hastened amongst others, to use the remain-

---

*The author means a convention of the people of South Carolina.

der of his power to take adroitly a multitude of military measures, favorable to the cause of which he was one of the ardent champions.* By his cares, the arsenals of the North were stripped of their arms for the benefit of those of the South; the little army of regulars was almost all sent to Texas; the navy was scattered in every corner of the seas. When the new power entered upon its functions, it found neither soldiers, nor marines, nor *matériel* at hand. In a word, the first steps of the rebellion were assured by the protection of the government itself, which had sworn the maintenance of the Constitution. The populations of the North, whose attention this culpable game did not escape, gave a fine example of their habitual regard for law, in respecting, under such circumstances, a government already smitten by the ballot, and so perfidiously betraying its mandate.

In the month of December, Congress met and heard a very carefully studied message from President Buchanan, but which was without conclusions rising to the exigency of the circumstances. Congress did not accomplish the preservation of the reign of the Constitution; and the efforts towards a compromise, made by some moderate and conciliatory men, completely failed.

The 20th of December the Convention of South

---

* General Floyd commands at this time a division in the army at the South.

Carolina passed, by unanimous vote, its ordinance of secession; and in all the States of the South warlike preparations were pushed with studied vigor.

At the close of December the war appeared almost inevitable; although it seemed, on both sides, that intimidation was sought to be produced by blustering threats, rather than a precipitation of actual hostilities. Innumerable meetings were held all over the country, at which the effort was made to prove, in the South, the full right of secession, and, in the North, its monstrous breach of law.

The intermediate or *border* States, Maryland, Virginia, Tennessee, Kentucky, sufficiently agreed in the opinion that South Carolina was going to work a little too quickly; and while declaring their sympathies for her cause, they thought that the time had not yet arrived for rending the Federal Constitution. It was necessary, they said, to see the new government at work, and to see it make the first attempt upon the Constitution, by carrying into act its famous Chicago platform on the question of slavery, before departing from the paths of strict right.

But, as it ordinarily happens when the passions are unchained, these words of sound reason, which were at the same time the notions of the better policy, were not heard; and certain incidents sufficed to set fire to the powder.

The port of Charleston is defended, amongst others, by two Federal forts—Fort Moultrie, on a peninsula of the coast north of the city, and Fort Sumter, on an isle in the middle of the pass. A small Federal garrison under Major Anderson held Fort Moultrie; and, while the secessionists of South Carolina were raising the pretension that this garrison should not be reinforced in any manner, Major Anderson, deriving inspiration only from his military duties, abandoned Fort Moultrie, and transferred himself with all his command to Fort Sumter, which furnished him a less threatened position.

There was a great burst of rage in the South against this act of provocation, so called; the North, on the other hand, resounded with applause for the "brave and loyal" Anderson.

By way of reprisal, the government of North Carolina took possession of Fort Macon, of Wilmington, and of the Arsenal of Fayetteville, which were without Unionist defenders. At this juncture it was necessary that General Floyd should retire from power; and he did so only after having pushed his boldness so far as to hold the weak President, Buchanan, responsible for the civil war which was about to break out, if he should not immediately recall the garrison from Fort Sumter.

In January, Mississippi, Florida, Alabama, and Louisiana also voted to secede. Virginia prudently stopped at the second step, and convoked, in her turn, a Convention to consider the same object. Missouri, Arkansas, Tennessee, followed the example of Virginia, and prepared to pronounce their vote on the first favorable occasion.

On the 14th of January, the Convention of South Carolina decreed that every attempt to reinforce the garrison at Fort Sumter, should be considered an act of war; and they pushed the construction of batteries designed to breach the Federal fortifications. The government of Mr. Buchanan, which, besides, had only a few weeks to live, recoiled before this menace.

On the 14th of February, 1862, the States which had already declared their secession, opened a Congress of delegates at Montgomery, in Alabama, which voted, four days after, a provisional Federal Constitution for the seceded States. They were then seven in number, to wit: South Carolina, Georgia, Florida, Alabama, Louisiana, Texas, and Mississippi. They were certain of soon seeing their number increased by Virginia and North Carolina, by Arkansas, by Tennessee, and by Missouri; and, according to the energy with which they should proceed, they reckoned still on the adhesion of the other slave States—Kentucky, Maryland, Delaware, and the District of Columbia, where the Democratic party had numerous members.

The Constitution of the Confederates is very similar to that of the Union. Slavery is better protected in it; the separation of the powers is a little less plain; the duration of the Presidential functions longer—six years instead of four. The right of secession is also reserved.

The 18th of February, Mr. Jefferson Davis, Federal Minister of War before Floyd, and Mr. Stephens, one of the most distinguished orators of America, were inaugurated as President and Vice-President of the new Confederacy.

During this time Mr. Lincoln quitted his modest abode in Illinois; received numerous ovations throughout his whole route in the North; adroitly baffled a conspiracy against his person at Baltimore; and arrived at Washington, where his administration was inaugurated the 4th of March.

One of his first cares was to take military measures, to guard against the effects of the weakness or the treason of the preceding administration. He caused several forts to be occupied; the arsenals to be refurnished with munitions; troops and vessels to be assembled; and, on the 8th of April, he notified South Carolina that supplies would be sent to Fort Sumter, by force, if necessary. Two vessels, in fact, left New York for that purpose.

It was still generally thought in the North that before this act of firmness the South would yield. They were deceived.

III.

FIRST HOSTILITIES.

After long conferences, it is true, hostilities broke out at Charleston. The secession troops, taking measures in advance of those of Mr. Lincoln, opened the fire of their batteries against Fort Sumter on the 12th of April, and, two days after, Major Anderson obtained an honorable capitulation.

A cry of joy seemed, at the news of this first deed of arms, to escape simultaneously from every Southern heart, to which responded a terrible burst of rage in the North. The struggle was decidedly inevitable. The cannon was about to speak, and to restrain for some time the object of public discussions to the single question, of knowing to what side should fall the intermediate States, which had not yet categorically declared themselves.

The 15th of April, President Lincoln issued a proclamation, calling to arms seventy-five thousand men,* and summoning the rebel States to return

---

* These seventy-five thousand men were distributed among the States according to the following scale:

Maine,	1 regiment,	of	780 men.	
New Hampshire,	1	"	"	"
Vermont,	1	"	"	"
Massachusetts,	4	"	"	"
Rhode Island,	1	"	"	"
Connecticut,	1	"	"	"
New York,	17	"	"	"

within twenty days under the flag of the Union. Congress was convoked in special session, as well as the Legislatures of the States, and, for some days, the journals were filled with proclamations, with orders of the day, and appeals for men and money.

At the South, response was made to these measures with not less ardor. Virginia proclaimed her secession the 17th of April, and Mr. Jefferson Davis announced the issue of letters of marque to privateers.

The 19th of April the Government replied with declaring the blockade of the coasts of the seceded States, and the 1st day of May, President Lincoln called to arms forty-two thousand volunteers for three years, and eighteen thousand marines.* Troops were

New Jersey	4	regiments of 780 men.
Pennsylvania,	16	" " "
Delaware,	1	" " "
Maryland,	4	" " "
Virginia,	3	" " "
North Carolina,	2	" " "
Tennessee,	2	" " "
Kentucky,	4	" " "
Arkansas,	1	" " "
Missouri,	4	" " "
Illinois,	6	" " "
Indiana,	6	" " "
Ohio,	13	" " "
Michigan,	1	" " "
Wisconsin,	1	" " "
Iowa,	1	" ". "
Minnesota,	1	" " "

* The first appeal had been addressed to the militia, raised for three months only; besides, several States refused their contingent. This second levy was distributed as follows:

concentrated at Washington on the one part, and at Richmond on the other; and the Potomac was thence, on this zone,* the limit between the belligerent parties.

The 20th of April, the Federals, not being able to extricate their vessels from the maritime arsenal at Norfolk, in Virginia, endeavored at least to destroy them; and sank, or set fire to the eleven vessels, among which were several frigates of great value. The secessionists succeeded in saving some of them.

It was not, however, until the end of May that the campaign was really opened. The Federals crossed the Potomac and proceeded to take possession, on the right bank of the river, of the city of Alexandria, and the neighboring heights of Arlington.

The troops of the North, under the general command of the venerable General Scott, were distributed at first into six corps: one at Fortress Monroe,

New York,	11 regiments.	Virginia,	2	regiments.
Pennsylvania,	10 "	Maine,	1	"
Ohio,	9 "	Maryland,	1	"
Illinois,	6 "	Connecticut,	1	"
Massachusetts,	5 "	New Hampshire,	1	"
Indiana,	4 "	Vermont,	1	"
Missouri,	4 "	Rhode Island,	1	"
Michigan,	3 "	Minnesota,	1	"
New Jersey,	3 "	Delaware,	1	"
Kentucky,	2 "	Kansas,	1	"
Wisconsin,	2 "	Nebraska,	1	"
Iowa,	2 "	In all, seventy-five regiments.		

N. B.—The regiments are numbered by States. They say the 4th Ohio, the 8th New York, &c.

* The author divides the country into five zones, running North and South.

in Virginia; one opposite Washington, on the Potomac; one in Western Virginia; one in Kentucky; one in Missouri; and one in Maryland.

IV.

SUMMARY OF THE PRINCIPAL MILITARY ACTS.

Not being able to give here a history of the military transactions, I shall limit myself to a brief indication of the principal ones.

The first affair of some importance took place the 10th of June, at Big Bethel, in Virginia, on the route from Fortress Monroe to Yorktown. About three thousand Federals, proceeding from Fortress Monroe and from Newport, attempted to carry the intrenchments before Big Bethel, and were repulsed after a sharp engagement, and with a loss of sixty men in killed and wounded.

Other actions also took place in Western Virginia during the months of June and July. One Federal division, among others, commanded by General McClellan, had notable successes in that quarter.

A more serious affair was the battle of Bull Run, or Manassas Junction, fought the 21st day of July. About twenty thousand Federals, under General Mc-

Dowell, advanced against Richmond by the route direct from Washington, by Fairfax Court House, Centreville, and Manassas. Between the last two localities, on the borders of the stream Bull Run, they engaged with the enemy, about twenty thousand strong. A combat, at first sufficiently sharp, turned subsequently into a panic on both sides, as often happens with troops for the first time under fire. But the panic was stronger on the side of the Federals, who ended by flying in great disorder as far as Fairfax, and even to Washington. They were not, however, long pursued; and they had, in all, four hundred and seventy-nine killed, one thousand and eleven wounded, and lost more than fifteen hundred prisoners. The secessionists had three hundred and ninety-three killed, and twelve hundred wounded.

The troops of the North, composed in good part of corps levied for three months, and the end of whose term of service had now arrived, could with difficulty be collected, and a considerable number of the militia returned to their homes. The Secessionists advanced anew to the border of the Potomac, but did not, whether from military prudence, or a system of policy, attempt to cross it. They believed their cause already gained.

The emotion which was excited in the North on this news, was, on the other hand, any thing but an indication of peace. Congress, called to take measures, decided upon a new levy, and this time upon five hundred thousand men engaged for three years.*

General Scott, who had, contrary to his inclination, and under the pressure of Congress, given the order for the march upon Richmond, chose to resign his command, and was replaced by one of the youngest generals of the army, General McClellan, who, while his colleagues were beaten at Manassas, was running to their aid across Western Virginia, and had made a brilliant and rapid march, with several successful engagements.

The victory of Manassas gave to the South its apogee of strength. Tennessee and Kentucky passed in majority to it. On the other hand, Western Virginia made a secession within the seceded territory, in order to remain faithful to the Union.

The campaign dragged along through the whole of the rest of the year 1861.

We may mention, however, as a remarkable occurrence, the battle of *Wilson's Creek*, in Missouri, the 10th of August, where the Federals had a thousand men *hors de combat*, of whom their chief, General Lyon, was killed, while the Secessionists had twelve hundred in the same condition. The result was undecided.

Another striking affair was that called the massacre of *Ball's Bluff*, the 21st of October, which pro-

* Distributed on a scale similar to that of the preceding levy, with the addition of the States of California and Oregon.

voked, with reason, an investigation, and was the subject of long controversy. About eighteen hundred Federals, under General Stone, crossed the Potomac at Edwards' Ferry, above Washington, on boats. Attacked on the other bank by superior forces, they were driven towards the river, were not able to re-embark, and were in great part killed or drowned. This design was so unskilfully conducted on the part of the Federals, that treason was charged to have had a part in the affair, and General Stone is still at this hour in prison.*

With the first days of 1862, the campaign reopened with new vigor, and everywhere simultaneously. The Federal army, about 600,000 strong, was, besides, seconded by a powerful marine, and the combined action of land and naval forces was seen to present itself at almost every point.

General Halleck, successor, in the West, of General Fremont, received the command of a large army, which was broken into six corps, and with which, seconded by a fleet of gunboats, he reconquered to the Union Kentucky, the greater part of Tennessee, a portion of the State of Missouri, almost the whole course of the Mississippi, and penetrated even into Alabama.

Sharp actions took place, amongst others, at the capture of Forts Donelson and Henry, in Tennessee;

---

* No charges were ever preferred against General Stone, and he has been liberated and assigned to duty.

at Mill Spring, in Kentucky, and finally, at Pittsburg Landing, near Corinth. At the last affair, the 6th or 7th of April, against the Confederate General Beauregard, there were about ten thousand men *hors de combat* on each side. The result was indecisive.

In the eastern part of the theatre of war, four maritime expeditions, besides the blockade, were directed against different points of the Southern coast, and afforded as results, the capture, amongst other places, of Roanoke Island and Newbern, in North Carolina; of Port Royal, in South Carolina; of some points in Florida, and of New Orleans.

The army called the Army of the Potomac, under the special command of General McClellan, advanced in its turn, at the commencement of March, from Washington on Richmond, as far as Bull Run. Then a curtain was let fall upon this front, while the mass of the army, passing by the left, embarked on the Potomac at Alexandria, for the purpose of landing at Fortress Monroe, and proceeding against Richmond by the peninsula of Yorktown.

On this new line of operations the Federals had advanced, after several successes, but with some degree of slowness, as far as within three or four leagues from Richmond. By the middle of June they might have been believed near capturing the secession capital, and there terminating the great war at a stroke, when the skilful movements of the Confederate generals, Jackson and Lee—who knew how to profit by their central position, and who had been crowned with success on the Shenandoah and the Chickahominy—succeeded in forcing the Federals to replace themselves on the defensive, and in wholly changing the situation.

While the Unionists had advanced in triumph everywhere simultaneously, keeping their corps hundreds of leagues apart, and getting in raptures over the conquest of certain points of very secondary importance, the Secessionists, whether by the force of circumstances, or by a good understanding of the principles of war, had concentrated themselves at Richmond.

They had thus been able to attack, in superior force, the army of McClellan, and to repulse it with great loss in different parts, during the Seven Days' fight. A furious action took place, from the 25th of June to the 1st of July, on the borders of the Chickahominy and of the James River, and did not terminate until the army of McClellan had been able to take a new base, and a strong defensive position on the James River, under the cannon of the Federal flotilla.

These events forced the North, still more persistent than ever in its determination to re-establish the reign of the Constitution, to a new levy, the fourth, and 300,000 men are in course of being recruited at this time.

From this brief chronicle of the principal military acts, one may already draw instruction perfectly in accordance with theoretic principles. It is, that if it is doubtless good for a country to defend with courage its very frontier, this country is still not lost for having allowed some points of that frontier to escape. That if, in a defence of Switzerland, for example, it should happen to us to have to evacuate, before superior forces, or menacing marches, cities as important for us as are to American Secessionists, Alexandria, Yorktown, Norfolk, Newbern, Port Royal, New Orleans, Vicksburg, Memphis, Nashville, Springfield, &c., this would not be a reason for our despairing, more than they, of being able to re-establish our power before our Richmond, which might be Berne, or some other of our central capitals.

V.

CONCERNING THE ARMY OF THE UNITED STATES OF THE NORTH.—STATISTICAL NOTIONS.—RECRUITING. — PAY. —ALLOWANCES.

I shall pass now to some indications more particularly statistical, on the subject of the military system of the United States of the North.

One of the finest operations which the Americans have effected, is, without contradiction, the creation, in so short a time, of their immense armies, which, in the last actions, have shown military capacities equal to those of the best troops in the world. The North, after the defeat of Bull Run, created an army of six hundred thousand men in from three to four months.

The United States had, before, only a small regular army of twenty thousand men, composed of the soldiery recruited by the Union, and employed essentially in the protection of the frontiers against the Indians. Aside from that, there were very numerous corps of local militia, but without organization, and existing rather on paper than as real effectives.

The new army was formed differently; and it is of it that I shall speak in what follows, taking more particularly, as an object of study, the army of five hundred thousand men formed by General McClellan.

The recruiting is entirely voluntary, and furnishes corps of two categories; the *regulars*, who have been increased by some regiments, to fill up the gaps created by defections, and raised only by the Federal authorities; and the *volunteers*, who engage freely for three years, or for the duration of the war, and which are furnished by the States. The volunteers are also divided into two classes: the State militia, which are the old local battalions, taken in mass and arranged on a war footing; and the regiments of the new formation, created for the occasion.

The *regulars* would correspond, then, to our *État-Major Fédéral*, and more particularly to its sections in the permanent service, and to our Federal corps of instructors and sub-instructors. The *volunteers* correspond to our troops wearing the cantonal cockades.

The mode of forming the volunteer corps is curious enough. They are at first the object of a sort of special enterprise. A patriotic committee assumes the undertaking, or an officer, holding a superior grade, raises a regiment at his own expense, and on his own responsibility. In order to do that, he opens recruiting offices, ordinarily for companies; he makes proposals, and stirring appeals in the journals; places placards at the corners of the streets; raises flags; puts inscriptions over the office, and sometimes has music. Then, when the recruits have reached the minimum prescribed by the official order, he passes them for pay, and to the service of the State, against the fixed allowances. The State, in its turn, passes the organized regiment to the service of the Union.

As in some old Swiss corps in the foreign service, the recruiting of a certain number of men insures a grade: thirty men for a commission of under-lieutenant, eighty for one of a captain.

This voluntary mode of recruiting, applied to the raising of considerable effective forces, is facilitated by democratic institutions and the habitudes of public life, without speaking of the mercantile spirit, which also mingles a little in the business. An excitement is raised by great popular meetings,—and there were, among others, two at New York which numbered not less than fifty thousand men, grouped around five stands; also by lectures in clubs; by the press, and by pecuniary advantages held out to the soldiers. Each soldier, besides his pay, has a right to a bounty of a hundred dollars. Lands will also be distributed, at the end of the campaign, as national rewards. The wives and the children of the soldiers receive an allowance during the time of the active service of the soldier: it is twelve dollars a month for a woman with two children. Lastly, the States, the cities, the corporations, add supplements to these bounties, even to the extent of doubling them.*

The pay is high in comparison with that of other armies, particularly that of the private soldier; that of the officer—especially of the mounted officer—who is at more expense in his charge, is not in the same proportion.

The following is a summary, comprising the allowance for subsistence, clothing, &c., for the officers, and not including the rations for the non-commissioned officers and for the soldiers:

Lieutenant-General, . . . 778 dollars per month.
Major-General, ... 477 " "
Brigadier-General, . . . 329 " "

* For the last levy the bounty was increased by two dollars, and by an advance in the soldier's pay and allowance. The State of New York adds to that fifty dollars; Boston, a hundred dollars. In some States there would be a question as to substituting this mode of recruiting by a conscription.

Colonels of Staff, of Engineer
Corps, and of Cavalry, . 237 dollars per month.
Colonels of Artillery and of
Infantry, ... 222 " "
Lieutenant-Colonels, . . . 198 " "
Majors, ... 179 " "
Captains, ... 120.50 " "
1st Lieutenant, ... 110.50 " "
2d Lieutenant, ... 105.50 " "
Non-commissioned Officers, " "
from 21 dollars to . . . 15 " "
Privates, ... 13 " "

The officers of the staff have from ten to twenty dollars per month more than the officers of infantry of the same grade. The Engineer Corps has also a higher pay than the other arms: it is, for soldiers of the first class, seventeen dollars per month: a sergeant receives thirty-four dollars per month.

The ration of subsistence is:

In money: thirty cents.

In kind: to the man, and by the day, three-quarters of a pound of pork or of bacon, or one pound of fresh or of salted beef; twenty-two ounces of bread or flour, or one pound of biscuit, or one pound and a quarter of corn-meal. Also a pound of potatoes to a man, threé times a week. Also for each hundred rations, eight quarts of beans, or ten pounds of rice. Also ten pounds of coffee or one pound and a half of tea; fifteen pounds of sugar; four quarts of salt; four quarts of vinegar; four pounds of soap; a pound and a half of candles.

The subsistence not received in kind is in the nature of allowances. The isolated soldier not drawing rations receives an allowance of seventy-five cents per day.

The ration of forage is:

In money: eight dollars per month.

In kind: fourteen pounds of hay, or twelve pounds of oats per day, or twelve pounds of corn or barley. Half rations of each are served.

The ration of straw is twelve pounds per month for a man, and a hundred pounds per month for a horse. In the field straw was not distributed. Hay was also more scarce than oats or corn. Bread was also generally replaced by biscuit, as more easy of transportation. With biscuit, the basis of the soldier's aliment is: bacon, beans, rice, coffee, and sugar.

The officers of the staff, even in the field, did not draw in kind, except the forage rations; they received the subsistence rations in money. Each staff formed one or more messes, transporting, themselves, their subsistence, or purchasing it on the route, when that was possible. The brigade commissaries furnished them at a fixed price.

VI.

EFFECTIVE FORCES.—DIFFERENT ARMS OF THE SERVICE.
—CLOTHING.—ARMAMENT.—EQUIPMENT.—MATERIEL.
—SUBDIVISION.

On the first of January, 1862, the Federal effective forces were reckoned as follows:

Regular Army.—Six regiments of cavalry, five regiments of artillery, nineteen regiments of infantry. —Total, with the corps of engineers, and the various staffs, 39,273 men.*

Volunteer Army.—Thirty-five regiments of cavalry (40,880 men); thirty-five regiments of artillery (65,-065 men); four hundred and thirty regiments of infantry (449,350 men); which, with the various staffs, give a total of 556,252 men.

The regiment of infantry is formed on the English system. It reckons only a battalion, or rather ten companies, which are left, at pleasure, in a single battalion, or are divided into two. In the latter case the lieutenant-colonel commands one battalion, and the major the other.

The regiments of the regular army were organized originally in two battalions, of eight companies each, with two majors to the regiment. They have now been placed on the same footing as the volunteers. The strength of the company, by the regulations, is

* Reduced to 25,000 men by defections on the part of the South.

from eighty-three to a hundred and one men. There were three officers to a company; but it has just been decided that there shall be a fourth.

The average effective force of the regiments on going into the field was about seven hundred men under arms.

The regiment is provided with music, which is ordinarily execrable.

The regiment of cavalry is composed of three squadrons, commanded each by a major. The squadron has four companies, the company ninety-five men at the maximum. Few of them exceeded sixty men on entering the field.

The regiment of artillery is divided into three battalions, commanded, each one, by a major; the battalion has four companies; the batteries six pieces.*

Among the special corps, a staff corps cannot be precisely stated, inasmuch as, properly speaking, it does not exist. It was not represented in the old army at all except by the topographical engineers, by the professors of the school of West Point, and by the inspectors-general. The functions of the officers of the staff are now filled by officers taken *ad hoc* from the corps or from civil life, and appointed, like the generals, by the Government. The greater part of

---

* The artillery is not organized by battalions, but by regiments of twelve companies, each company constituting a battery of four or six pieces.—(*U. S. Artillery Officer.*)

the European officers who have taken service under the United States have been employed as staff officers.

The engineer corps is furnished by the regular army. One company of pioneers, chosen from the different corps, is formed in each division. The corps of engineers of the regular army reckons only seven to eight hundred men, comprising therein the officers, of whom there are two colonels, seven lieutenant-colonels, sixteen majors, twenty-two captains, &c.*

The commissariat is formed of officers taken from the corps, or of civil functionaries. This service is a little at a disadvantage (*en souffrance*), and suffers from the fact, among others, that commissaries filling very important functions, commissaries of divisions and of army corps, have only subaltern grades. Having all the care of the supplies and their transportation, their task is very important in a country often without roads and without subsistence, and where the armies have to draw after them immense trains. From thence easily arise abuses, and I might properly remark, on this occasion, that there is a great excess of military baggage in the army of the North.

The ordnance corresponds almost to the staff peculiar to the artillery. It is a department which is charged with the work of the arsenals and the foundries. It reckons a regular corps of about five hun-

---

* The corps of topographical engineers having been merged into this corps, its organization has been changed.

dred men, at the head of which is a colonel, and to which have been added a great number of volunteers and laborers from civil life, to supply the pressing needs at the entrance on the campaign.

The medical corps is composed of military surgeons and those in charge of the hospitals, assisted by civil surgeons, by volunteers, by nurses, &c. This service is also at a disadvantage, although the Government devotes to it the greatest anxiety. The churches are generally used as hospitals; besides, at Washington, there have been constructed for the same use extensive frame buildings, furnished with every desirable comfort. Several large and sumptuous vessels serve as hospital boats; the ambulances (*cacolets*) are after the French system.

The signal corps is a department of the staff peculiar to the United States, and which has assumed considerable importance there. By means of flags by day, and of colored fires by night, it communicates simultaneously with the marine and with the several corps. It is an application of the usages of fleets to the land service; and has even acquired sufficient development to furnish scope for productive industry. A large manufactory of night-signals of this kind, the Coston manufactory, of New York, even exports its products to Europe. By night the patrols recognize one another by lanterns and rockets with colored fires; and by their changes of shade they form the words of the countersign. For the same purpose, each division of the army has its distinctive colors, marked by a special flag remaining with the staff of division.

There are also attached to the staff, balloonists, telegraphists, printers, topographers; mechanics and engineers for the use of railroads; photographers and *estafettes*, without reckoning multitudes of journalists and private historians, who obtain, very improperly, the authority to follow these operations, and who receive forage rations.

The dress of the army is simple and practical, as is suitable for an army created solely for the campaign. It varies according to the States, but it does not differ widely from that of the regulars, which has served as a standard. It is a deep blue frock-coat; has one row of yellow buttons; is loose; is worn ordinarily, when out of service, open, with a vest; pantaloons of the same color; cap of the same color, and of form similar to ours, but higher. A long sack-coat serves as the garb in quarters. Each man has, besides, a heavy great-coat, with a large cape falling back on the coat. Some corps, amongst others, of the Western States, have the hat of black felt, with wide brim, in place of the cap.

Other regiments, particularly of New York and Pennsylvania, have costumes a little more fanciful. There are red Zouaves, blue Zouaves, gray chasseurs, green sharpshooters, with variations of cut and of color more or less picturesque, and with sounding names. A New York regiment, the Lafayette Guard, has the classic uniform of the French line; another, of the *chasseurs à pied* of the imperial guard. The mounted corps of artillery do not differ sensibly from the others, except that they have the jacket very short.

The distinctive marks are the gimp on the arms, for the non-commissioned officers. As to the commissioned officers, they had formerly the epaulette, sufficiently massive; to-day it has been replaced by wide bars, crosswise on the shoulders, with border and ornament in silver and gold.

The ground of these straps (in English, shoulder-straps), by its color indicates the arm; the embroideries indicate the grade, to wit: a bar of gold at each extremity for the lieutenants; two for the captains; a gold leaf for the majors; a silver leaf for the lieutenant-colonels; a silver eagle, in the middle of the straps, for the colonels; a star for the brigadier-generals; two for the major-generals (generals of divisions); and three for the lieutenant-general (general-in-chief).

Besides, the coat of the subaltern officers has one row of buttons; that of the superior officers and generals, two rows; in pairs of two for the brigadier-generals, and of three for the generals of division.

There is also worn in actual service the crimson scarf, *en sautoir*, or crosswise.

The pantaloon of the officer has a cord on the exterior seam, of color corresponding to the arm of service.

The pantaloon of the non-commissioned officer, a stripe the color of that of the respective corps.

The arming and equipment suffered at the outset from the deficiency of the arsenals and the magazines, plundered by the men of the South. But the manufacturing power of the States of the North soon remedied the evil.

The arm of the infantry is the rifled musket. There are all models of them, but the pattern styled the English now prevails. European commerce has furnished a good part of them; the rest are made in the United States. One arm peculiar to this army, is a five-shooter rifled revolver (Colt's) which has been given to some regiments, and which has been much praised.

The cavalry is armed in part with the carbine; others with a revolver, which is worn in a leather holster fixed to the sabre-belt, a little behind the right hip.

The equipment is, for the greater part of the corps, the belt with the cartridge-box and bayonet. Many regiments have, however, the sabre bayonet at the belt, and the cartridge-box attached to the shoulder-belt passing crosswise under the waist-belt.

All the straps are black, and the general aspect of the troops is gloomy. Each soldier has a knapsack with the articles of dress, and a small equipment, variously composed; as a blanket, a bag for bread, a metal bottle covered with cloth, a pair of boots, and a tin cup.

The officers wear high boots over the pantaloons, which is less a prescription than a necessity, in a country often muddy, and where they do not often take the trouble, even in the approaches to the large cities, to pave the ways.

Some regiments have the large tents for eight or ten men, which follow with the baggage of the regiment; others have the shelter tent, on the French system, more or less modified. One of the principal modifications consists, for example, in the white sheets being replaced by black ones, of India-rubber cloth, which offers the double advantage of being lighter and superior against rain, and of not being perceived so far by the reconnoitring parties of the enemy. In America it is not much dearer than white canvas. The mounted men have a large piece of gum-cloth, with an opening in the middle, serving at once as cloak and blanket,—very convenient for rainy weather. Each artillery carriage has also its cover of India-rubber cloth.

The saddlery has a particular character. The new regiments, and the greater part of the mounted officers, have a saddle invented by General McClellan, as the result of careful study in Europe and in America, and which, in the opinion of experts, unites all the excellencies of the different systems for a campaign saddle. Among other things it is very convenient for packing, and does little injury to the horses. It is composed, altogether, of two side panels of wood joined, leaving the back free, by means of a peculiar arrangement of hoops and straps. The stirrups, on the Mexican model, are of wood, and covered in front with a band of leather, which rests against the end of the foot without engaging it, and protects the lower part of the leg against rain and the spatterings of the mud. There are no pistol holsters, the revolver being worn, as I have already said, at the belt, but instead two pockets for various supplies.

The *matériel* of the artillery has also suffered disadvantage from the spoliation of the arsenals. A special manufactory has been provided for a good part of it, and has made, amongst others, all sorts of cannon, more or less monstrous, for pieces of position. The calibres are now without limit; and the styles are so numerous that it would be very difficult at once to make an exact classification of them.

For the navy, have been constructed rifled pieces of one hundred and of two hundred pounds, modifications more or less fundamental of the Whitworth and Armstrong guns.

The field-pieces are:

1st. Old French eight-pound howitzer guns, called Louis Napoleons, in bronze, and of smooth bore.

2d. Twelve-pound pieces, and twenty-four-pound howitzers, of bronze, smooth bore.

3d. Four-pound pieces, and rifled eight-pounders, on the systems of Parrott and Rodman, of iron.

In the reserve artillery are used rifled eight-pounders, twelve-pound cannon, smooth bore, and twenty-four-pound howitzers.

The artillery of division is composed ordinarily of three rifled batteries of small calibre, and one battery of eight-pound howitzer cannon. A battery of regulars is attached to each division, and the commandant of this battery commands also the artillery brigade of the division.

The Rodman rifled cannon is a piece of wrought iron, in hoops, with five grooves, with conic projectile, having the lower end of lead, of eight or nine pounds for the field calibre, and of thirty-six pounds for the siege pieces.

The Parrott cannon, more improved, is a cast-iron piece, widened at the breech, of from three to ten grooves, according to the calibre. The small calibre of the piece called the four, because it corresponds to that number of the smooth bore, has a projectile of eight pounds. There are some of them of the weight of two hundred pounds, requiring a charge of from fifteen to eighteen pounds of powder. The Parrott projectile is furnished with a copper covering.

There are also Dahlgren cannon, Lincoln mortars, James' howitzers &c., &c.; but I should not undertake to enter on a detailed description, not being sufficiently sure to avoid confusion and errors. Among the curious innovations which free competition has brought to light, I have seen a rifled field cannon, designed to be pushed instead of being drawn, by its team. The axle of the carriage is furnished with a double plate of sheet iron, serving as a parapet to the artillerists, and with a range of pikes in front to operate as bayonets.*

The Federal forces are subject to the orders of the President of the United States, who exercises the chief command through the medium of the Secretary of War, or of a lieutenant-general, or sometimes directly. I am obliged to say *or*, for, in the actual state of things, it is difficult to know upon whom rests the superior direction of operations.

General Scott, after Bull Run, was replaced by General McClellan, and the latter, once confined in the peninsula of Yorktown, was not replaced by any one. After the recent reverses on the Shenandoah and the Chickahominy, General Halleck was called from the West to the post of General-in-chief at Washington; and it appears to be he who now

---

* It would be scarcely possible to collect more errors in so small a space.

The *matériel* of the artillery has suffered *no* disadvantage from the spoliation of the arsenals; *no* special manufactory has been provided for a good part of it; calibres are *not* without limit; and the styles are neither very numerous nor difficult to classify.

The one-hundred-pounder and two-hundred-pounder rifled guns for the navy are Parrott guns, such as are used in the army, and are *not* fundamental modifications either of Whitworth or Armstrong guns.

The artillery of division is *not* ordinarily composed as stated. The number of batteries attached to a division of infantry depends entirely upon the numerical strength of the division; one, two, or three pieces to one thousand men, as depends upon circumstances. The proportion of rifled to smooth-bore batteries depends also on circum-

commands, or rather directs in chief the operations, in concert with the Chief and the Secretaries of the Government, who, in their turn, are controlled by the military committee of the Senate, and by Congress, whose intervention in the conduct of the war is daily. Numerous political tribunes, besides, as well as the imperious declamations of clubs, and of a licentious press, have often also too considerable an influence over the employment of the military forces. It follows that the chief command is in truth the weak part of the army, and this duty the most at a disadvantage, while, however, no one in particular can be accused—this vice appertaining to the very institutions of the country. It is, however, aggravated in the present case by the accidental circumstance that

stances—the smooth-bore, instead of the rifled, being generally in excess.

There is no "Rodman" *system* of artillery in the United States service. Major Rodman, of the United States Ordnance, invented and perfected a method of casting guns of large calibre, which is applied to existing "*systems.*"

There are neither "*four-pounders*," "*Lincoln Mortars,*" nor "*James' Howitzers*" in the service of the United States Artillery: nor is every artillery carriage furnished with a cover of India-rubber cloth.

The *field-pieces* of the United States service are the light twelve-pounder (smooth bore), and the wrought iron rifled gun of three inches diameter of bore, the latter weighing about eight hundred pounds, and throwing a projectile weighing about ten pounds.

Twenty-pounder and ten-pounder Parrott guns are *temporarily* used in small numbers; as are also occasionally the twelve, twenty-four, and thirty-two-pounder howitzers—relics of a former system.

A cast iron gun of four and a half inches diameter of bore, throwing a projectile weighing about thirty-two pounds, is the ordinary regulation *siege* gun.—(*U. S. Artillery Officer.*)

neither the President nor the Secretary of War is a military man; that the Secretary of the Navy is not a seaman; that there are no officers in the military committee of the Senate, and that the two great political parties of the North wage an incessant war against the most conspicuous generals.

The Federal forces have been distributed into several armies. There were formerly two principal ones—that of McClellan in Virginia, and that of Halleck in Tennessee; and a secondary one under Frémont in Western Virginia. Besides, there are also three strong detachments on the Atlantic coast, and five or six others here and there.

Since the first days of July, there have been, besides the detachments, which are a little less numerous, it is true, three principal armies.

1st. That of the Potomac, which would now be better called that of the James River, under General McClellan, to the southeast of Richmond, 90,000 men.

2d. That of General Pope, before Washington, in the direction to Richmond, about 50,000 men.

3d. That of General Grant, formerly of Halleck, at Corinth, in the south of Tennessee, about 50,000 men.

These different armies are divided into army corps of two to three divisions of infantry and one of cavalry.

The division reckons ordinarily three brigades of infantry and one of artillery.

The brigade of infantry reckons ordinarily four

regiments, performing the service of the line and of chasseurs.

The regulations for manœuvring the different arms, and of the field service, are generally imitated from the French rules, of which they are often a literal translation.

The regulations for the internal service, the administration, and the manual of arms, are reproduced rather from the English system.

Amongst the military publications outside of the regulations, may be cited, amongst others, a work of General Halleck on the military art, which has merit in regard to judgments upon strategy and grand tactics. General Scott and General Casey have published elementary books upon the subject of infantry. General McClellan has published a work on the cavalry service, and two volumes of studies on the European armies, which he visited at the epoch of the war of the Crimea, being then captain of engineers. Major Delafield, also delegated to the Crimea, has published a book on engineering, and on the art of war in Europe, very rich in statistical information. The greater part of the most useful French military works are reproduced in extracts, or translations entire into the English language, and serve for the instruction of the officers: as the Art of War of Jomini; the Staff Manual of De Rouvre; the Memorial of Laisné; the Institutions of Marmont, etc.

The maps and plans prepared by the topographical

engineers are generally fine works, which, besides, are executed with rapidity. Topography, it may be observed further, is a science much appreciated and widely diffused in the United States. The periodical reviews, and even the daily journals, accompany all their narratives of military events with plans and sketches, some of which are occasionally valuable, and all have a merit of seasonableness, of which the army often takes advantage.

By spring, the divisions of the Army of the Potomac were properly instructed and disciplined in the manœuvres. It is true that they had been eight months receiving instruction, and that in circumstances calculated to develop the aptitude of soldiers. The cavalry, amongst other arms, considering the fine race of horses and the natural boldness of the men, is excellent as light cavalry and for foraging. To make a reconnoissance, or an adventurous raid, it would not yield in any thing to the best cossacks of the Russian army. Expeditions, sustained for twenty leagues over frightful roads, or across woods, rivers, and marshes, by day and by night, constitute the ordinary service of a good number of the regiments.

The general information of the men in all which concerns encampments, and the establishment of routes, bridges, and abatis, their patience and their *sang froid* under disappointments, their force of will, and their persistence against obstacles, are truly remarkable. On the other hand, the etiquette of discipline, the respect for authority, and the good order of the internal service, fall short of what is desirable.

There is wanting also the spirit of cheerfulness and gayety which sustains so happily the *morale* of the weak at trying moments. The conduct and the character of the American soldier have something of sadness, of reserve, and of silence, which is precisely the opposite of that which is met with in the European armies. The song and the laugh there are the exceptions. It is true that the soldier is at the same time a citizen. He thinks of his country and of his party; he talks politics; he reads almost every day the gazettes brought to the camps by intrepid little carriers; he has family cares; he receives and writes many letters; he often sends a correspondence to the journals; he communicates military impressions to the Senators of his State, and his plans of campaign to chiefs the most elevated in grade. Few knapsacks of the private soldier would be found unprovided with a complete apparatus of secretary, paper and envelopes of different sizes, collections of postage-stamps, blotting-paper, etc. I have often borrowed from the first comer the materials for my correspondence.

If the American soldiers are not gay in their disposition, it is not, however, through contempt of alcoholic stimulants. Intoxication is a vice too common, and so excessive in their ranks that many indulge in it even to the extent of falling on the spot by the side of their guns. Whence arises this injurious consequence, that from fear of the abuse of spirituous liquors, it becomes necessary to prohibit even the moderate use, and that their sale at retail is interdicted to the sutlers, as well as at the stores of the garrisons.

Amongst the qualities which are also wanting, ought to be mentioned that sentiment of fellowship and of fraternity in arms which contributes so much to give confidence and solidity to the character of an army. Individuals and corps live there a little too much for themselves, seeing, often, only a rival where it would have been proper to see a friend and a brother in arms. This defect can be easily comprehended and excused in a country making but the commencement of its apprenticeship to a military career, and where all the institutions and the habitudes of civil life have hitherto reposed on the largest allowance possible of individual liberty.

On the other hand, this same spirit of liberty, of individuality, and of constant rivalry, which has so strongly developed artificial contrivances adapted to aid man in his daily struggles against nature,—mechanic industry, among others, and machinery of every species,—contributes also its advantages to the army.

In no other army, for example, are the railroads of a use so important and so frequent.

They have used them in the South for skilful strategic combinations, and, on both sides, they have daily employed them for tactical movements of the greatest boldness, sometimes for transportation under fire of the enemy, for *estafettes*, and even for reconnoissances and scouting expeditions.

At the time of the recent evacuation of the White House, the 28th of June, the Federal General Stoneman, commandant-in-chief of the cavalry, advanced by way of exploration and as a scout on a locomotive, in the direction of Richmond, in order that he might be able to communicate directly and promptly the signal to fire the provisions which there was no longer time to carry away.

In another reconnoissance of the most adventurous character, some time before, two officers, as brave as intelligent, of the staff of General McClellan, the Count de Paris and the Duke de Chartres, requested, on the route, a locomotive, and, climbing upon it, they were able to explore promptly the country, and to bring back, in one morning, news of the enemy acting at the distance of fifteen leagues from head-quarters.

The construction of new railroads, their destruction and their repair, play a very grand part in this war.

The telegraphs are managed with not less boldness and activity. In the army of the Potomac, for example, the staff of the general in command rarely stops more than two or three days without being connected with all its divisions, and with the Government at Washington. Whether it were on the boats at anchor in the bays, or in the midst of the marshes of the Peninsula of Yorktown, or in the bosoms of thick forests, while the routes were not even traced for the wagons, one could see rising all around him the network of wires with wondrous rapidity. More than one officer of the staff has recovered his direction in the forests of Virginia by means of the posts, or the trees truncated for this purpose, of the telegraphists,—and the latter have often unrolled their wires as rapidly as the army marched.

The telegraph connected not only the various fractions of one and the same army, but also the different armies themselves together, through the medium of the central office at Washington. The Government had thus at each instant, and at pleasure, news of the operations over many hundred leagues of extent.

The balloons were frequently employed with success for reconnoissances; and during their station above the forests masking the ground, they were sometimes put in communication with the head-quarters by a telegraphic wire. A scout of this novel kind rendered, amongst others, signal services to General McClellan during the battle of Fair Oaks, the 31st of May.

Field printing-presses, operating with great celerity, are also attached to various staffs. As for any thing further on this head, the printing-press is more connected with the manners and customs of the American people than with those of any other. There is not a village which has not its printing-press and its journal. A head-quarters, as populous as many a village, might well pretend to the same privilege. I subjoin here, Mr. Counsellor, a specimen of the elegant pamphlets which our printers executed for us in the marshy woods of the environs of Yorktown. I should add that these pamphlets, and the telegrams, simplify greatly the labor of the staff department.

But all these improved engines are, after all, but accessories; and if the directing thought of the operations is not up to the height of its task, they only complicate it for him. The facilities of execution aggravate the faults of conception more frequently than they aid in correcting them. In many circumstances, it would have been very desirable for the army to have fewer telegrams at its command, and to be more independent of the political fluctuations of Washington.

VIII.

ARMORED VESSELS.

Since I am to speak of machinery utilized for the war, I shall be pardoned for saying, also, a few words of one of the most remarkable facts of this war, viz.: the transformation in naval constructions.

We may well wait for what the mechanical genius of this people may realize, having reference to the means of the struggle, as well as the remarkable innovations in other more pacific domains. The results have still surpassed the anticipations. The old wooden navy, those colossi of 120 guns, which made the pride of England and of France, are now only decayed powers in the presence of the heavy calibres and the armored vessels created by the Americans.

The two belligerent parties had from the commencement of the war constructed vessels covered with iron, of various forms, and on each side they hoped to surprise one another. On both sides they found themselves gradually entering the lists with equal arms.

The 6th of March, in Hampton Roads, near Fortress Monroe, one of the strangest naval combats took place—one with which the whole world has resounded. The secession frigate, the Merrimac, proceeding from Norfolk, had just attacked, and disabled in a few hours, two powerful frigates of war of the United States, the Cumberland and the Congress. The next day a vessel equally singular in construction, the Monitor, in its turn entered the contest on the side of the Federals, and forced the terrible vanquisher to a retreat.

Having had the advantage of seeing these two vessels, and of visiting the Monitor in the very roadstead of the combat, I shall endeavor to give here a brief description of it.

The *Merrimac* has nothing particularly remarkable in fact, except her iron armor and ram. She is an old frigate of the first class, of the United States. She was of very small cost, and made in 1857 her first voyage to England. Anchored at Southampton, she was then remarked upon by critics for her proportions and for the cut of her hull, and provoked controversy amongst seamen and builders.

Sunk by the Federals at the time that they were engaged in evacuating their maritime arsenal at Norfolk, where she was, she was afterwards put afloat again by the Secessionists. They razeed her, and covered her with iron plating, rising by plates superposed one upon the other, in the form of a roof above the deck. They furnished her with ten Armstrong guns: four at each side, one on the prow, and one on the poop. In front was fixed an enormous iron ram; by the ports, and by two openings near the chimney, were arranged pipes for throwing boiling water and steam, as a defence against attempts at boarding.

When the Merrimac wished to go out, thus armed, for the first time, she could not float, and was obliged to be lightened; but she remained always slow in her movements. Only once was she able to use her ram at pleasure; this was on the occasion of her demonstration against the Cumberland, which once experienced her destructive power. Since then, her adversaries have always been able to avoid her blows.

The strength of this vessel, as the engagements at Hampton have demonstrated, consisted chiefly in the resistance which her armor opposed to the enemy's fire, and which permitted her, without fear, to moor herself with broadside presented, at short range. She confronted thus three complete broadsides of the Cumberland, a sustained fire from the Congress at short distance, and another of the Monitor. This last succeeded only in inflicting upon her an injury in front, which caused her to abandon the struggle. To supply the rapidity of movement which she lacked, the Merrimac went escorted by two or three steamers and gunboats, performing about her the service of scouts and sharp-shooters.

At a distance, the heavy-looking Merrimac, without mast, and with her low chimney, gliding slowly over the sea, had a strange and monstrous aspect, which struck the inhabitants of the coast with superstitious terror.

It is known that this vessel was destroyed the 18th of May, at the time of the capture of Norfolk by the Federals. The Secessionists not being willing to let her fall into the hands of her former proprietors, and not being able to carry her away, inasmuch as she was then receiving repairs, blew her up while evacuating the place. On the other hand, they towed to Richmond the carcass of another Merrimac, whose early appearance on the James River has been announced.

4*

The Monitor, created by Captain Ericcson, is of a wholly different character. It was constructed after a plan well considered, and with the idea of offering the least possible surface to the blows of the enemy; of giving to this exposed surface a solidity proof against every thing; and of causing the density of the water to operate as a shield for the most delicate parts.

Entirely answering to this plan, the Monitor makes but little show, and it was some time before I was able to discover her at Hampton Roads, in the midst of the vessels of every dimension confided to her protection.

Upon the whole, this vessel is a raft, like a body on a level with the water, under which is found a hull, less long and less wide, enclosing the machinery, and with the spiral line of the hull, the anchor, and the helm all below. On the raft is raised a tower, sheltering two Dahlgren cannon of two hundred pounds each. The tower can be moved on a circular framework, and this movement is directed from the interior of the tower. By this means the cannon, while remaining all the while under cover, can be brought to bear in every direction of the horizon.

The raft has a length of about one hundred and seventy feet by a width of forty, and a depth of five, of which three and a half are under water. Her waterline is elliptical.

The lower hull is about one hundred and twenty feet in length, thirty-five in width, and seven in depth.

It is perceived then that she is curtailed at the points of the ellipse by fifty feet, and on the sides by five feet, on the full length of the raft. These two parts are of oak, covered with sheets and plates of iron. The tower, wholly of iron, is nine feet high by twenty in diameter, and presents a thickness of metal of nine inches, in eight concentric walls. The two ports are three feet above the deck. Her mechanism for effecting the rotation of the tower is very ingenious, but would demand, in order to give a complete idea of it, a detailed description with drawings, which I have not the means of presenting here. Two men alone suffice to handle the guns. The smoke escapes by traps in the roof of the tower, and also by means of a ventilating apparatus which conducts it to other grated traps under the deck. Apart from the tower, the raft offers no other prominent point except the pilot-house, also of iron, which rises twelve inches above the deck, and has inclined sides. Holes, covered with glass, allow the pilot to direct the vessel, while being fully under cover.

It is thus seen that this battery is theoretically adapted to its object; its delicate portions are covered by a great thickness of water, and its exterior portions, of small surface, strongly protected, and circular, offer little hold for the action of the projectiles. Practical experiment corroborated these calculations of theory. In the combat of the 7th of March the two guns of the Monitor contended for two hours against the ten of the Merrimac, without other damage than a blow at the look-out of the pilot-house. Several times did the Monitor, manœuvring with ease, avoid, without ceasing her fire, the charges of the ram of her antagonist.

Since then the *Monitor* has not been engaged but once, against Fort Darling, below Richmond, and it was admitted that she required still some improvements, among others the following:

1st. The arrangement of the guns in the tower does not permit a sufficient inclination of range;

2d. Her slight elevation above the water-line causes it to be doubted whether she can bear the open sea. Room would also fail her for supplies for a long voyage;

3d. The tower has the ordinary inconvenience of casemates; the smoke, and especially the heat, are not dissipated there with sufficient readiness, and soon become very annoying to the gunners.

These observations, the first two in particular, will appear the better founded, as Captain Ericcson had not had the intention of making the Monitor any thing else than a coast battery, designed originally, during the incident of the Trent, to defend the entrance to the harbor of New York. The constructor having afterwards solicited the opportunity of proving his battery against the enemy, she was sent in haste to Fortress Monroe, when the real existence and the approaching sortie of the Merrimac were learned. The guns which were used in the fight were not of the intended calibre; and Commodore Dahlgren thinks that if his gun, of large calibre, had been in action, the Merrimac would have been pierced and sunk.

The fight of the 7th of March produced a great sensation in the United States. The two vessels engaged in the tilt, which until then had been considered as chimerical constructions, and on which many a jester had exercised his wit, were surrounded with respect, and on all sides mechanicians, ship-owners, and engineers put themselves to work to create and improve vessels of this kind. They used old vessels which they improved; they constructed new ones; they invented others, of forms more and more odd; and to-day the navy of the United States possesses a whole fleet of these formidable engines. The Naugatuck and the Galena were the first to join the Monitor in the James River. The waters of the Mississippi bear also a fleet of them, and, very recently, the Secessionists have put one afloat, the Arkansas, which made her *début* in passing by force the Federal gunboats, in order to strengthen the defences of Vicksburg.

It is necessary, however, to recognize, that these so improved products of the mechanic arts bear in them defects, arising from their very excellencies. The smallest error in time, a slight accident to the machinery, is sufficient, sometimes, to paralyze the action of an immense force, and to cause disappointments which are so much the more lively as the hopes excited have been great. It is thus that, at the attack on Fort Darling, the 15th of May, the Federal flotilla was unable to obtain any result. The Galena, which had been grounded in ascending the James River, had to be lightened, and was soon deficient in munitions. The Naugatuck saw her hundred-pound gun burst at the first fire; and the Monitor had to remain at long range to get her angle of aim.

At the same time that it was sought to appropriate these new means of destruction, each party aimed with not less eagerness at obtaining the corresponding means of preservation. After the poison, the antidote; after the projectile, the plate: thus is the career of invention pursued. This second search is also not less interesting than the other.

I give below the facts of the contest which I have heard the most appreciated, in view of new combats between the Merrimac and the Monitor.

Against the Merrimac, the North proposed to employ the shock, as being the most effectual mode of action. Certain enormous steamers, of great swiftness, and heavily ballasted, amongst others the Vanderbilt and the Constitution, were to rush, under a full head of steam, upon the Merrimac. The latter, less capable of moving, could not avoid the shock of one of these steamers, and, according to the calculations and the laws of dynamics, would necessarily be sunk. With this object, a flotilla of this naval cavalry was for a long while in station below Fortress Monroe, always under steam. While it should have prepared and executed its charges, the Merrimac would have been entertained by the fire of the Monitor and other armored vessels.

Great success was not expected from boarding, considering the difficulty of throwing men on the inclined sides of the armor, who, besides, could be driven back by jets of boiling water and steam.

Against the Monitor, I have heard it said that the seamen of the South thought, amongst others, of three means, which appear in fact susceptible of some efficiency.

They would attempt to board her, and bold men would throw shell into the tower through the ports. But the Monitor put herself on guard against this danger by the arrangement of pumps of boiling water discharging at the ports.

Or, they would open the deck and sink her, by a bomb-shot of heavy calibre, and as vertical as possible. But such a shot it is difficult to make.

Or, to capture her with a chain,—to throw it in the manner of a *lasso* around the tower, and to ground her on the coast.

It is unfortunate that these different means, sufficiently curious, of contest, cannot, perhaps, be put to the proof, in new actions between these same two vessels. But they will be so, without doubt, in others, under conditions very similar.

Upon the whole, the navy of the United States, whether it be by its creations or by its operations, has acquired, and is acquiring still, the greatest honor in this war. It may well console her for the disappointments which the land army has experienced.

The blockade of so great an extent of coast, a blockade which, whatever may be said of it, is as real and as effective as a blockade has ever been, testifies the power and the vigilance of the Federal fleet.

The actions of Fort Pulaski, of Forts Donelson and Henry, of Port Royal, of Hampton, of Vicksburg, of New Orleans, and of other points of the Mississippi; also of Pittsburg Landing, and of Harrison's Landing, show what resources of energy, of precision, and of intrepidity, there are among these brave seamen.

In fine, the frequent transportation of troops, successfully effected at the distance of hundreds of leagues along the coast, the embarkation and disembarkation of the Army of the Potomac, of those of Burnside, Butler, and Sherman, with all their supplies and *matériel* of the heaviest calibre, prove that the most difficult and extensive operations can be seriously undertaken by an army, as well as seconded on all the navigable waters.

At this time an entire fleet of vessels, identical with the Monitor, is in course of construction in the various ship-yards of the North, without reckoning a great number of others on different models.* When

* Amongst other variations from the system of Capt. Ericcson, is

these different vessels shall have taken the sea, that is to say, in a few months only, the United States will possess, for the moment, the greatest military naval force in the world, and will be able to exercise sovereign control over their waters. I have it from a very experienced and impartial seaman, that the famous *Warrior*, or her rival *La Gloire*, would find themselves at a disadvantage against a single Monitor. In return, those vessels are more suitable, it is true, for distant navigation.

In the course of this year, nine new Monitors, constructed under the direction of Capt. Ericcson, ought to be launched, to wit: the Montauk, the Catskill, and the Passaic, in course of construction at Green Point, New York; the Sangamon and Lehigh, in construction at Chester, Pennsylvania; the Nantucket and the Nahant, in construction at Boston; the Weehawken, in construction at Jersey City; and the Patapsco, in construction at Wilmington, Delaware.

At the commencement of the year 1863, the military marine of the North should reckon fifty mailed vessels, on different systems and of different strength.

The South, really very inferior in this respect, and everywhere closely blockaded in her ports, is also making great efforts to establish for herself a navy.

mentioned the system of Whitney, of which a specimen, the Keokuk, is at this time being built at New York. As capable of resistance as the Monitors, it will be lighter, inasmuch as wood enters, for a great part, into its construction, and be more manageable. It will have a speed of ten knots an hour.

It is said that two new Merrimacs are already in advanced construction at Richmond, and that they ought soon to make their appearance in the waters of the James River. Another is expected to contribute to the defence of Vicksburg, on the Mississippi. Others are in construction at Charleston, and still others are receiving their armament in England, designed to give chase to the commercial vessels of the North.

IX.

SOME PERSONAL IMPRESSIONS IN REGARD TO THE AMERICAN AND SWISS ARMIES.

I shall now take the liberty, in terminating this report, to sum up, under the form of observations or *desiderata*, some of my personal impressions on the defects of the American Federal Army, and then to indicate some comparisons which I could hardly prevent myself from making between that army and our own.

The two armies have, indeed, in many respects, a great resemblance, and are a little deficient, it is necessary to avow, in the same particulars. They are both more or less composed of armed militia of confederated States, of citizen soldiers accustomed to liberty, embarrassed with civil business as well as family cares, and living under republican governments.

Owing to a great number of causes, but particularly to the trad'tions of the middle ages, to engaging in foreign services, and to a permanent danger, resulting from disagreeable and too powerful neighbors, Switzerland possesses, if not a strength, at least a military spirit substantial and active, a sentiment completely unknown hitherto to Americans, who have prided themselves rather in not being military in any thing. But apart from this fact, there are, unfortunately, too many defects common to the two countries, and to the two armies.

As to what concerns the American Federal Army, the principal causes of inferiority are, in my opinion, the following:

1st. From lack of authority in the generals, in consequence of the exigencies and the vices of democratic institutions, which protect all the restraints upon the vigorous and wise conduct of the war,—intrigues of parties in the government and about it; excessive personal ambition; sordid flattery of the soldier-voters; the systematic aspersion or commendation by the press, of the several generals, according to the party to which they belong; exaggerated fears on the part of the government of seeing the rise of future military dictators; the superabundance of clubs, of journals, of tribunes, which, without wishing it, furnish valuable information to the enemy, and facilitate, in a singular manner, the business of spies.*

* Without wishing to replace the liberal system of government of

2d. The defective mode of forming the army. The system of voluntary recruiting by the inducements of the pay, or by the stimulation of political passions, furnishes a great number of individuals more or less depraved, or inept for the valuable service of the field, but who are admitted, to make up the number. The rest of the nation, thinking they are doing enough in aiding to raise pay for these *mercenaries*, find themselves too little interested in events, do not feel sufficiently their burden, and do not take in the war an interestas serious as the circumstances would demand. In the great cities, at New York, Philadelphia, Boston, and even in the face of the enemy at Washington, amusements go on as in time of entire peace;—they dance, they dine, carry on festivities, boast loudly, and, what is more serious, they know

the United States by a despotic régime, it might yet be required in time of war, that military exigencies should be more seriously regarded, and that the very object of the war should not be rendered more difficult, if not even impossible to be attained, by an exaggerated political *doctrinarianism*, which consists in wishing to respect every institution, and every individual right, created for times of peace. I could cite here, with advantage, the example of Switzerland, as jealous, certainly, of its democratic prerogatives as are the United States. In 1847, at the time of the campaign of the Sunderbund, General Du Four, Commander-in-chief of the Federal army, began by demanding of the journals an entire abstinence from remarks on the subject of military affairs. Through the medium of the diet and the cantonal governments, the press was seriously invited to be silent on the events of the campaign, and not to reproduce any thing but official acts which should be transmitted to it by the governments, publishing bulletins for this purpose. The army and the country found the advantage of this measure, which could be put in execution in the United States as easily as in Switzerland.

not how to sacrifice on the altar of the country in danger, any rancor, or any political purpose. The contest of parties and of cliques pursues its ordinary course, and even more intensely than in ordinary; many a Republican abolitionist of the North rejoices more over the reverses of a Democratic general, of McClellan, for example, than over his success. The Democrats do the same in regard to the abolition generals, as, for example, Frémont. If the army were recruited by conscription, or if each citizen, subject to service, were held to military duty, as in Switzerland, the various classes of society would be more equally and more directly identified with the war, and would better comprehend the necessity of the sacrifices which it demands.

3d. The mode of recruiting furnishes a great number of bad officers, having sometimes no other title to their commissions than having known how to entice a few recruits to inns or clubs. It is particularly injurious when that happens, as it too often does, alas! in regard to the positions of the superior officers. For two good officers taken thus from the ranks of the orators, or from the magistracy, there are five or six of them completely incapable in the face of the enemy. Being from that time let into the secret that military knowledge is not the first condition to obtain an officer's commission, every influence is brought to bear to effect the nominations. The ties of relationship, of friendship, of party, considerations of speculation even, cause to be named for very important positions men totally incapable of filling them. When that happens in the staffs, where the service, necessarily indeterminate and not susceptible of being regulated as in regiments, does not betray the incapacity of the officer until after the act, the hurtful consequences which may ensue may be easily understood. I do not wish to cite here proper names, for that would not serve my end; but it would be easy for me to prove what I advance, by facts too palpable. I should add that, owing to the intrigues of parties, and the compliance of the press, it is often difficult for the public, even for the Government and the superior officers, to ascertain whether such an officer is a pretender, an adroit actor, or a man of merit. The conscription would give better men for the troops, and would allow a choice exclusively military for the officers.

4th. This state of things has still a bad consequence: it is, that the officers of the same corps, divided often by politics, have not always the moral confidence which they ought to have in one another. That state of things presenting itself in the staffs, generals are seen to distrust their own *aides-de-camp*, and the latter to distrust one another; whence a system of petty mysteries, very injurious to the service. It may be said that, owing to this cause, added to others, there does not exist a staff really organized. Thus marches and operations are too often made in almost complete ignorance of the movements and of the strength of the enemy, or much too slowly.

5th. The regiments are too numerous, and too weak in effective force—a defect proceeding from speculation, and from the mercantile spirit mingling in the matter of the recruiting. To obtain recruits, recruiting officers are necessary; and to dispose of the latter, there must be numerous corps. It is not only a great expense, involving a pure loss of superior officers, and of staffs of regiments, but also a waste of men taken from subaltern functions, where they could be more useful. In consequence of the same principle, or rather of the same abuse, there are (will it be believed?) no dépôts for regiments! When reinforcements are needed, new regiments are ordinarily raised; and thus they have always either entirely conscripts or decimated veterans. How much more advantageous would it not be in all respects to introduce, on the other hand, the new recruits into the fractions of the regiments which have already had experience! But there would be fewer places for officers to bestow, fewer favors to be distributed, less aliment for political intrigue! That would not be the interest of the greater number, and, unfortunately, men of mark also, thirsting for popularity, conform their sentiments to those of the multitude.

6th. The corps, like the staffs, have far too much baggage. The punishment is often produced, without doubt, in the fact that it is left on the way; but there ought to be a general rule to reduce it in a uniform manner for the success of operations, often shackled by this immense train of *impedimenta*. There are regiments of infantry of 600 or 700 men, which draw after them as many as twenty wagons. The staff alone of General McClellan had not less than thirty wagons. Some contained, it is a fact, armchairs, beds, and a crowd of useless articles. I hasten to add, that the honorable general did not require so many for himself, and that he gave, on the contrary, in his whole person, the example of a modesty and a severity unfortunately little followed.

7th. The military zeal of the army is not excited by any advantage proportioned to the dangers. No honorable distinctions, no decorations or pensions, not even retiring pensions, are assured to the wounded, or to the widows and orphans.* Then the music is wretched; the uniforms gloomy; no distribution of brandy; and a severe prohibition against making booty. There is only patriotism and the pay to stimulate the boldness of the combatants. But this is not enough in the present case to lead men reso-

* A pension law has always existed for the American army. Many have been enacted at different times, the most recent being the "Act of Congress approved July 14th, 1862." Appropriations for "Medals of Honor," to be given to "those who distinguish themselves in action," have been authorized by the "Resolution of July 12th, 1862," and the "Act approved, March 3d, 1862."

Appointments to the vacancies in the regular army are made *only* from the graduates of West Point, and the *distinguished regular non-commissioned officers and privates.*—TRANSLATOR.

lutely to death. As for the pay, that is gained in advance, and if one is thrown out of service, the pay is lost for himself and his heirs. As to patriotism, it is that of a civil war, and the sad struggle of the parties which we have mentioned in the very camp of the North, blunts, or gives it a false direction. If it has its moments of dash, it has more often still its fainting-fits.

8th. The very organization of the discipline is fundamentally defective, in that it transfers too much to the military service, where obedience above every thing ought to reign, the individual privileges of the citizen, who prides himself essentially on being free. Courts of inquiry and courts-martial, for example, are multiplied to infinity, diverting, at every turn, a good number of soldiers from active service, without aiming, most frequently, at any result. Veritable lawsuits, bristling with incidents of every kind, are always pending by the dozen in each division, in which the question, in the greater part of the European armies, would be one of the simple competence of superior or general officers. Heaps of pamphlets, besides, result from them, which there is a custom of sending to all the corps, and the transportation and dispatch of which by the officers, is done sometimes to the detriment of important business.

The officers have too little the habit of using their disciplinary power, and make too many concessions to the whims of the soldiers. There are many provosts charged specially with the police, but they have no armed police or special corps under their orders, and the surveillance is very difficult. The abuse, or fraudulent use of leaves of absence is not either sufficiently prevented, or severely enough punished. A troop which is near the great centres of population, and to railroads, and which does not believe the situation critical, has often even a third part of its effective force absent, by abuse of leave or without leave, some on parties of pleasure, others on clandestine visits to their families.

This same spirit of individual independence, so laudable in civil life, but whose excess is so fatal to military discipline, is found in every thing, and at all times. In the cabinet of the generals, and in the matter of the operations, it introduces itself into discussions, conferences, too frequent councils of war, and assumes the initiative and the decision of the responsible chief. The orders have not habitually the character of precision and of authority which they ought to have; one does not perceive in them sufficiently the nerve of command; they are often also followed, in place of execution, by replies, by observations, and sometimes even by protestations on the part of the officer who receives them. The official instructions and orders might be taken for diplomatic notes. They negotiate, much more than order and obey. Upon the whole, they do not sufficiently believe in the rights of superior authority, and in the fact that a penal military code can be seriously applied. It will be so, probably, so long as there shall not have been made some examples of the guilty in high places.

9th. Finally, the North is still affected by a cause of inferiority in a certain peculiarity of its strategic checkerboard; its Capital, Washington, the capital of the Union, which it wishes to restore, is located on the very frontier; and the care and the defence of this important and eccentric point attach to it great, very great considerations of preference.

This city is, in fact, so well covered against Virginia by the Potomac,—here about three-quarters of a league wide, and accessible to the Federal gunboats,—that it is in as great safety as if it were ten leagues in the interior, and is not really threatened except on the side of Harper's Ferry. It is, then, behind this last point that there ought to have been constructed a great intrenched camp. It would have served to flank the capital, to watch the passages of the Potomac, and to keep the army in a central position, whence it might be able to debouch at pleasure, in front by the Shenandoah, to the right by Western Virginia, or to the left by Washington. In place of that, the capital has been made the military centre; it has been surrounded by an immense belt of works on both banks of the river, extending even beyond Alexandria, works, the guard alone of which absorbs and throws out of action a very considerable number of troops, and whence it is impossible to debouch by land except on a single line of operations, and without secrecy. Thus, each time that the Northern troops have been put *en route* from this point they have been anticipated—whether at Manassas, in the peninsula of Yorktown, or in the valley of the Shenandoah, —by the concentrations of the enemy.

Nothing proves better than the military events which have occurred in Virginia during this war, how much the choice of a bad base can weigh with a fatal burden on all the operations of the campaign. The principal faults, and the most acute disappointments of the Federals, have been, for the most part, only the natural consequences of this first error of having taken for a base a point so eccentric as Washington, and which ought not to have been considered any thing but a good *tête de pont* of advanced posts.

Approaching, now, some points of comparison between the American Federal army and our own, I shall present eight observations:

1st. The army of the United States asserts the principle, that the soldier ought to be able to subsist on his rations, without being obliged to disburse a fraction besides. I believe this a very good principle, and, whether it be in regard to the justice of the matter or in regard to health, it ought also to be practised in our army. To maintain the health of the soldier, it is necessary besides, that his food be not too different from that of the civilian. I think, then, that it would be well to add to our present rations a ration of coffee and of sugar; a little more bread, and regular rations of different vegetables, for the evening meal. The porringer of the soldier should be of sheet iron, capable of withstanding the fire, and serving in extremity as a coffee-pot.

2d. If we should ever be under the necessity of arming our frontier lakes,—as it was proposed to do in public discussions at the time of the purchase of the Radetzky, and in the instance of the annexation of Savoy to France,—or should we only have to fortify their banks, we ought not to forget that vessels of wood, and light walls, can no longer hold out against the heavy calibres and iron plates of the American system, which are already imitated by the European powers.*

3d. With a climate as variable as ours, it appears to me as urgent here as it does everywhere else to renounce the bivouac, and to furnish the troop with a tent. I shall make reference, on this point, to the Report which I have already had the honor of addressing to the Swiss Military Department in August, 1859, on my return from Lombardy, limiting myself

---

* The principal States of Europe have sent instructed and intelligent officers to the United States, to study there the innovations on the military domain called out by this war. I am persuaded that, in many respects, and especially in regard to rifled arms, carbines, and cannon, to the armor of ships, and various machinery, Europe will bring back good fruits from the experience of America.

to recommend anew its conclusion, that our *élite* troops should, at least, be furnished with the shelter tent on the French system. With the view of making this provision, it would, perhaps, be advantageous to make some experiments with India rubber, or with some impermeable fabric, but of deep color. The shelter tent appears to me so much the more urgent in our army, as our soldiers have not, as others have, any covering for the ordnance.

4th. The late experience which I have had in America of the wants of the troops in the field, have confirmed me in the conviction which I had already, after the Italian war, that spades, axes, and mattocks are articles of the first necessity, and of daily use in all the corps. It would, then, be very desirable that means should be taken in advance, of having a sufficient provision of those articles, in case of our army being put into the field.

5th. The saddle called the McClellan saddle, with the method of replacing the pistols and their holsters by a revolver at the belt, would be worthy of an attentive consideration, at this moment particularly, when this question is under discussion, and when a new saddle is proposed for our cavalry. I should remark, in passing, that our castings complicate the saddlery, take up valuable room, load the horse, and that when one is not in the saddle, he finds himself unarmed.

I much hesitated whether I should not bring to

Switzerland a specimen of the McClellan saddle. Unfortunately, the trouble and the expense of transportation prevented me,—so much the more, as, had I commenced to make purchases, there are many other models of military results which I should have desired to be able to submit to the Department.

6th. Switzerland has always been distinguished by the speciality of the *aim*. The address of our riflemen, become proverbial and justly celebrated throughout the entire world, constitutes a notable portion of our strength, although there is some abuse, perhaps, whether amongst ourselves or abroad, in regard to the real importance of very fine marksmen in the field. It is, however, proper not to allow ourselves to be outstripped by other countries, or at least not to have the reputation of being so, and, consequently, to follow the improvements which are made elsewhere. America has much contributed heretofore to the improvement of the rifle. To-day she has gone farther, and has armed many regiments with a rifled revolver of five shots, of which I have heard many favorable remarks, and to which I believe I should draw the attention of the Department.

I should be perhaps inclined to doubt the advantages of this arm for precision of aim, the certainty of which demands more calmness than rapidity. But for choice battalions, or for a select company in a battalion, for the head of a column in case of a brisk attack, or for a defence against cavalry, it is necessary to recognize that the fire of a battalion or company, being capable of being delivered five times in succession, and promptly repeated, will certainly be of great advantage. At all events, the fact of the existence of this arm, with which three regiments of the North are furnished (and in one, the Burdan regiment, is one Swiss company, formerly commanded by M. Trepp of the Grisons, at present a major in the same corps), has appeared to me to merit being remarked upon, at least as an interesting curiosity. The price of this rifle is from two hundred and fifty to two hundred and sixty francs.

7th. As to what concerns distinctive marks, what I have seen in America has not failed to remind me of the discussions which have taken place in Switzerland on the retention or the abolition of the epaulets. Personally, I was then in favor of retaining this badge for officers. To-day I am forced to recognize the fact that the epaulet becomes almost untenable in the field. I doubt whether, in conditions similar to those in which we found ourselves in the United States, epaulets would have lasted three weeks. Thus, whatever might still be the regulations for the old army, nobody wore them. At the end of some weeks, we were forced by the difficulties of transportation to diminish our baggage and appendages, and it is probable that, if epaulets had been worn, they would have been got rid of on that occasion. Perhaps one day it will be so in Switzerland! I am therefore of the opinion that this occurrence should be foreseen, and that, if the discussion on this point should break out again, we should think of proper insignia for the war footing, while keeping the epaulets, since we have them, for the peace footing and for schools.

8th. I have also experienced that a certain variety in the costume of the infantry corps, as is seen in the volunteer regiments of the different States, does not injure the good style of a division or of a brigade, and, besides, facilitates the service, provided that there is uniformity within the regiments, and general uniformity of arms and equipment.

The varieties of uniform allow a corps, a wing, a disposition of troops, to be more easily recognized, and by their means one can more easily put himself right than by the numbers on the caps. They facilitate the recognition of the corps after an engagement; aid in the discipline and the police; and contribute, also, to excite emulation among the different corps.

I conclude, hence, that it is more hurtful than fortunate, that we should have made such great efforts in Switzerland to arrive at so complete a Federal uniformity in the matter of dress, and that the fear of oddity should have engendered an excessive competition among the cantons in this respect, causing us to fall into the contrary excess; that if the question should again come under discussion, and some cantons should wish to intreduce modifications in the costumes of their battalions of infantry, we ought to be very careful how we prevent them.

For the special arms, on the other hand, instructed by the confederation, and by small cantonal detachments, the subject would possess inconveniences, without presenting the same advantages as for the infantry at the time of large concentrations of troops.

Such, Mr. Federal Counsellor, is the information, and such are the observations, which I have thought proper to submit to you. I shall be happy should you deign to find in them something useful for our Swiss soldiery; and I am wholly at your disposal, to add to them further indications which may be judged necessary, and which I may be in a position to give.

I have the honor to be, Mr. Federal Counsellor, with the most profound respect,

Your very obedient and very devoted servant,
FERDINAND LE COMTE,
Federal Lieutenant-Colonel.

LAUSANNE, *August 9th,* 1862.

SUPPLEMENTARY REPORT.

Mr. Federal Counsellor:

I should add to the above report some supplementary remarks, drawn from the important events which have transpired in America while these pages were passing through the press.

During the second half of the year 1862, the war was continued with a vigor more and more marked, but with chances so divided, that matters are almost in the same situation as at the opening of the campaign last spring. If the North, on the whole, has made some progress in the recovery of territory, if it has succeeded in holding some of the points conquered by its arms, it has, in return, lost a notable portion of its prestige and of its moral power; for this progress is far from answering to the display of force, and to the importance of the sacrifices which it has been necessary to make.

Great battles, great in the numbers of the forces engaged, and in the losses, if not by the combinations, have been fought, without ever giving to either side great military results. That is owing, in part, to the temperament of the troops, who have more tenacity than dash. The conqueror ordinarily becomes weary after the conquest, which prevents him from giving a decisive blow. Besides, the numerous watercourses, and the accidents of the ground, almost always offer to the vanquished, in these conditions, a means of putting himself under protection against a sanguinary pursuit.

It is necessary, however, to recognize the fact that the operations of the generals of the South indicate more strategic sagacity amongst them than among their adversaries, or, at least, that their strategic combinations can be better brought to a successful execution than can those of the generals of the North. In the South, the country, more united, inasmuch as it is defending its firesides, more ardent for the struggle, has arrived, by the logic of the situation, and by the community of inflamed passions, at a sort of dictatorship, which seconds the action of the superior officers. Success in arms is the first law. The North has, on the contrary, all the embarrassments of a Constitution, and of a formal regard for law to maintain. While the South can order and require at need, the North must discuss and negotiate.

For the naval expeditions, and for the transportation of the troops along the coasts, the North requires long parleys with the constructors of vessels; and the same is the case with the railroad companies, with the bridge-builders, and with the furnishers of subsistence. These preliminary negotiations, all the delays of which are never calculated beforehand, always hinder the execution of the best conceived plans of the generals of the North, and have caused the failure, amongst others, of the two principal strategic movements combined by them in Virginia.

On this portion of the theatre of the war, by far the most important, matters are almost in the same state as last spring, indicating, however, slight advantages on the side of the Federals, who have advanced, altogether, from the Potomac beyond Bull Run, and to the Rappahannock, and from Fort Monroe to Yorktown, which they still hold, although having been compelled to evacuate the greater part of the Peninsula.

After the long battle of the Seven Days, at the end of June and the commencement of July, General McClellan remained some time in his position on the James River, while they were discussing, at Washington, the best mode of opening the arrested campaign, and of resuming the offensive.

The first measure, of a new levy of 300,000 men, ordered the 2d of July, by President Lincoln (already mentioned above), was followed by the call of General Halleck to the post of general-in-chief of the armies of the Union. That officer came to Washington to take the direction, by the telegraph, of the numerous armies and fractions of armies scattered over the whole territory of the Union.

Halleck had had incontestable successes in the West. His army had brilliantly reconquered Kentucky and Tennessee; he had gained the battle of Corinth, the 6th and 7th of April; but it is just to reproach him, after that, with having taken too passive a position; with not knowing how to entertain the rebel army of Beauregard; and with having, finally, allowed the latter to escape, a great part of which, having arrived at Richmond, was in time to aid the Secessionists on the Chickahominy against McClellan. If the latter had reverses, Halleck was in some degree the indirect cause of them.*

The first care of the new general-in-chief was to reunite the different armies operating in Virginia, and this idea was assuredly very laudable. The concentration could be effected in several ways: either by withdrawing the army from the peninsula of Yorktown to the front of Washington, or by reinforcing it. On each of these fronts there were equally three lines of operations to choose, whether it were wished to ad-

---

* The author has naturally fallen into this error from the general opinion entertained at that time. It is now known that no reinforcement except a few fragments was sent to Richmond from this army, after its evacuation of Corinth, which the wooded and marshy nature of the country rendered it impossible to prevent. Corinth was occupied by the Federal troops immediately upon the heels of the rebels, who were as hotly pursued as the nature of the roads and wooden bridges would permit.

vance by the right, in front, or by the left,—that is to say, along the Blue Mountains, by Manassas, and by Aquia Creek; or yet, by York River, or by either bank of the James River.

These six alternatives presented in reality almost equal chances of success. The question was solely in knowing how to adopt promptly one of them, and to execute it with vigor; to carry upon one of these lines a mass of from 130,000 to 150,000 men, while leaving upon the others detachments sufficiently troublesome to drive the enemy to dispersion. Upon the whole, the best of these alternatives was that which offered the simplest and readiest means of execution, and, in so far as I am able to judge of the matter, I incline to believe that the concentration by Aquia Creek, and by land towards the Rappahannock, was the preferable. Unfortunately, the time, that most precious element yet in war, as in commercial affairs—in which, however, the Americans know how to recognize its full value*—this time was consumed in long parleys, and in veritable diplomatic conferences on the part of the North. The concentration was decided to be made in front, from Washington towards the Rappahannock and Culpepper, which was in my opinion very wise. General Pope assembled there, the middle of

* In the United States the maxim, *Time is money*, has passed into a proverb. It is seen inscribed over the front of many counting-houses, and over the doors of offices. With more reason still, should be put on all the standards of the staff, as well as on the front of the office of the Minister of War, the variation: *Time is victory*.

July, the three corps of Banks, McDowell, and Sigel; but it was only towards the middle of August that these forces began to be reunited to those of the Peninsula, by the evacuation of Harrison's Landing and the re-embarkation of McClellan.

The generals of the South were not so tardy in deciding, although they did not, any more than the others, act with all the celerity possible. Leaving McClellan under the surveillance of one portion of their forces, they conveyed successively the rest of their army to the rencounter with Pope. Already, the 9th of August, Jackson had checked Banks at Cedar Mountain. The following day's engagement took place in the environs of Culpepper, where the Rebel cavalry of Stuart displayed much boldness. On the 18th, Pope put himself in retreat; the 22d, a turning movement of Stuart attacked his rear at Catlett's Station, while Jackson threw himself out by the Blue Mountains as far as the environs of Manassas, where his sharpshooters appeared the 24th, in the evening.

It might have been thought that General Pope, who, on assuming his command of the Army of the Potomac, had issued very eccentric orders of the day, in which, among other things, he affected a sovereign contempt for *lines of retreat* and *bases of operations*, wishing, he said, to establish his head-quarters in the saddle,—it might have been thought, I say, that General Pope would not be much alarmed at the enterprises of Jackson and Stuart on his flanks and rear, which were more audacious than really dangerous. He was wrong, doubtless, not to have sufficiently strengthened his right, and to have neglected to occupy the defiles of the mountains; but there was a good remedy for that by means of the troops which were still on the Potomac, and by means of those whom he could have sent thither himself. Having, besides, a second base at his disposal, at Aquia Creek, on the Potomac, where the corps of Burnside was then disembarking, and where it was necessary that the army of McClellan should disembark, he had no cause for great uneasiness. On the contrary, he ought to have been rejoiced to see the enemy offering suddenly such fine opportunities for his advantage, manifesting the rash project of placing themselves, by the route of the mountains, in the *cul-de-sac* formed by the army of the Federals on one side, and by the elbow of the Potomac on the other. The prospect of a Napoleonic victory offered itself to General Pope, had he allowed these movements to be developed, and had he kept a little to the system of war and *sangfroid*, of which his proclamation had excited the hope. In place of that, he thought only of one thing, not to lose his connection with Washington. He sacrificed every thing to this puerile fear, and caused the mass of his forces to make a retrograde movement towards Manassas, thus driving away the troops which, having disembarked at Aquia Creek, desired to join him, and had marched with this object towards the upper Rappahannock.

The 27th, 28th, 29th, and 30th of August were employed in a succession of engagements, as disorderly as bloody, about Manassas and Centreville, in which several corps deported themselves very bravely, but in which it is impossible to find amongst the Federals any directing thought, any united action, any other object than that of regaining as quickly as possible their route to the bridges of Washington, threatened by the bold partisans of Jackson and of Stewart.

It was altogether different on the side of the Confederates. They had found a mine of success, which they worked with incredible good fortune even to the last vein. They had seen, on the 9th of August, Pope becoming excessively alarmed at the movements on his right; they continued to act in this direction, and found no reason for departing from a system which succeeded so well for them. Four times, at intervals of twenty-four hours, they broke out from the mountains on the army of Pope, precipitating his march, deranging his front, and providing themselves with no retreat except in the fear which they inspired in the Federals on theirs. In this way the latter were forced back, still fighting, even in sight of the Potomac, which they reached the 1st of September, still engaging that very day in a very spirited fight between Fairfax Court House and the river.

During this time the troops of McClellan, comprising therein the corps of Burnside, had disembarked at Aquia Creek; some had been conveyed to Fredericksburg, and still held the Rappahannock during the fights at Manassas; others had sought to rejoin Pope towards Bull Run by land, and had, in part, arrived there; others had been re-embarked to convey themselves more in the rear of Alexandria. From this city, to which McClellan had also directed himself, the corps were thrown out as rapidly as they debarked, towards Centreville and Fairfax, to the succor of Pope; and it was they which, arriving very seasonably, sustained the last efforts of the retreat commenced after Cedar Mountain.

For a moment, the 29th of August, General McClellan had only a few regiments about him at Alexandria, and the government at Washington, making complaint against him for not having arrived sooner for the desired junction, reduced him officially to the sole command of the troops immediately in hand, while all the rest were put under the command of General Pope. But in three days the wheel of fortune made a complete turn. The 2d of September McClellan was named commander of the defences of Washington, and as all the troops rallied in this direction, he was re-established, four days after, at the head of the entire active force, General Halleck remaining all the while general-in-chief of all the armies of the Union. Pope was immediately sent to

Minnesota, where a terrible insurrection of the Sioux Indians had broken out.

The concentration which General Halleck had wished to effect on the 12th of July, took place at length, at the commencement of September, under the walls of Washington, and after rude checks. Some garrisons had been left by McClellan in the Peninsula, amongst others, at Yorktown and Williamsburg,—a very wise measure, providing for the future the means of more easily debouching on Richmond in that direction, in case they should wish to undertake it anew.

Arrived on the border of the Potomac, the Confederates, under the general orders of General Lee, did not think proper to stop in the midst of so fine a career. They had two courses to take to continue the offensive, which they had so favorably begun. Either to carry the works which are regarded as protecting Alexandria and the bridges of Washington, and there capture a considerable portion of the Federal army, hemmed in by the Potomac; or to continue their manœuvres by the left, turn the Unionists, cross the river up stream, and penetrate into Maryland. The first course, which would have been much the more advantageous, was not attempted by the Secessionists, thus affording ground for the observation, already often made, that young troops easily exaggerate the strength of the works of fortification with which they meet in their movements. The works on the heights of Arlington and of Alexandria, as little dangerous as they might be to an enemy possessing the boldness which the Confederates had just shown, produced an effect much above their real importance, and stopped short the Confederate army. Lee judged that his troops were better for marching and for pushing adventurous designs than for fighting in line and in a manner somewhat regular, as it would have been necessary for him to do in the face of the intrenchments. He preferred the trifling glory of an invasion of Maryland to the attempt, which might have been so fruitful, of an attack upon the *tête de pont* of Washington. He threw himself back by the left towards Harper's Ferry, crossed the Potomac the 4th and 5th of September, between that point and Washington, on bridges and at various fords, and advanced on Frederick City in Maryland. He thence threatened Baltimore at the same time as the Federal city, but he also left on his right the whole army of Washington, and, behind him, several Federal detachments holding the garrison at Harper's Ferry and other positions on the Potomac.

It is evident that such a design could not have any real military advantage, but the recent successes of the Confederates might well excite in them some illusions; besides, they flattered themselves with being able to bring to their cause, by this stroke of boldness, the slave State of Maryland, and with seeing the population rise in their favor. They were deceived in this expectation, and, spite of their gentle treatment of the inhabitants, the latter received the Secession flag with a coldness almost general.

On the other hand, General McClellan put himself in pursuit of the invaders, or, to explain myself more correctly, he proceeded to encounter them, judging, without doubt, and with reason, that it would be sufficient to attack this army with some degree of vigor in front, to drive it back on the Potomac, and, there engaging it during the passage of the river, the result could not fail to be decisive. The chances presented themselves so much the more favorably, as the Federal garrison at Harper's Ferry, reinforced by the garrisons on the retreat from Winchester and environs, amounted at this time to as many as twelve thousand men. Such a force ought to be able not only to hold with certainty the place, and prevent the rebels from using its bridges, but also, in case of extremity, to detach some thousands of men against Lee, to aid in his capture or in his total defeat when he should be hemmed in by the Potomac.

The event did not prove thus, whether owing to the skill of the Secession generals, to a little too much slowness on the part of McClellan, or to the remarkable cowardice of the Federal chiefs at Harper's Ferry.

It was not till the 10th or 11th of September that the Federal army, disorganized by the reverses of Pope, could make a decided movement from the environs of Washington; and the five or six days lamentably lost in the cares which were indispensable, perhaps, for the material condition of the troops, were used to good advantage by Lee. His advanced guard, under Hill, after having proceeded as far as New Market, took position behind Frederick, in the defiles of South Mountain, while the corps of Jackson carried on an active siege against Harper's Ferry, by both banks of the Potomac,—a siege which commenced on the morning of the 13th. The 14th, McClellan chased Hill from South Mountain, after a hot engagement, which took place within hearing of the cannonade of Harper's Ferry, at the distance of four leagues. The Confederates fell back from South Mountain in the direction of Sharpsburg, on the Antietam creek, followed closely by the Federals, and took position behind the hills of Antietam creek. The 17th McClellan resolutely attacked them, and on this day was fought the severest battle of the war. The circumstances for twenty-four hours had greatly favored Lee. The chiefs of the garrison of Harper's Ferry had ignominiously capitulated on the 15th, surrendering to Jackson more than ten thousand prisoners, and an immense *matériel*.*

* It is consoling to mention here that one thousand cavalry, commanded by Captain B. F. Davis, recalled by this circumstance the fine feat of the sergeant of Minden. Not wishing to surrender without trying their fortune to the end, they made a sortie by Virginia, bravely traversed all the enemy's lines, ascended the Potomac, and proceeded to cross the river and re-enter Maryland in the very rear of Lee; capturing from him, besides, a part of his baggage.

Without losing a moment in estimating his booty, Jackson had parolled the prisoners and had brought back to Lee two divisions, which, inflamed with success, were in the highest degree useful on the day of the 17th. McClellan had to act against a stronger force than he had thought; it was necessary for him to display all his resources to succeed only in gaining the field of battle, and in forcing the Confederates to retreat. To proceed beyond that was not possible for him; he had himself suffered too much. The day of the 18th was given to the care of the killed and wounded, as well as of the *matériel*, while it would have been necessary, in order that the action of the previous day should be truly fruitful, to be able to recommence the attack with fresh vigor. The 19th, Lee quietly recrossed the Potomac, after having left about twenty thousand men in Maryland, and having caused his adversaries to lose still more. Harper's Ferry was reoccupied by the Federals the same day, and the river remained for some time the limit between the two opposing armies.

About three or four weeks were passed in observation on the Potomac, enlivened only by skirmishes, and with attempts without great importance on either side. The Confederates, however, accomplished a very prodigy of boldness. Two thousand men of Stuart's cavalry, commanded by their intrepid chief himself, crossed the Potomac the 10th of October, on the extreme right of the Federal army, near Williamsport; advanced into Maryland, and thence into Pennsylvania as far as Chambersburg, where they made a raid according to the most approved rules; then turned to the southeast, and, making the complete tour of the Federal encampments, recrossed the Potomac at their extreme left, re-entering Virginia by Edwards' Ferry. The whole was accomplished with loss of only a few men.

The Unionists, on their side, usefully employed this time in the organization of the new levies. Besides the three hundred thousand men under command at the beginning of July, the President had secured, on the 4th of August, a new levy of three hundred thousand men for nine months, which should be furnished, if found necessary, by a draft, by lot, or by a regulated conscription.

On the invasion of Maryland, a hundred thousand men had been spontaneously put on foot by the States of Pennsylvania, Maryland, and other States of the North.*

Until the recruits could be organized into regiments and disciplined, and the old regiments filled up and reformed, the lost *matériel* replaced, the army, in a word, restored to a good war footing, there was no

---

* From the beginning, a strong repugnance was manifested in almost all the States for the conscription. The greater part of them, as also the cities and the various corporations, preferred to give extraordinary bounties to volunteers. These bounties amounted to as much as three hundred dollars, in addition to the one hundred dollars of the Government.

hurry, in a purely military point of view, for resuming the offensive. Without doubt, if the Federal army, in its turn, had been able at this moment to throw promptly a strong mass on the communications of the Confederates, by Aquia Creek or by the peninsula of Yorktown, and to advance on Richmond, while the chief part of Lee's force was still facing the Potomac in the valley of the Shenandoah, a fine operation would have been realized, and without the loss of a minute. I am not sure but it should have been attempted, and that it would not have met with some success. But, as has been seen, plans of campaign of some magnitude are slow to be elaborated in the army of the North, and slower still to be put in execution. It is probable that the project would have been so timed that Lee would have been able to paralyze it, by a concentration in front of the Capital. In renouncing, therefore, an operation of this kind, and declining to enter the lists by the very front of the enemy,—that is to say, taking the bull by the horns,—the North had nothing better to do than to await the reinforcements of its new levies, and the putting in action of all its resources. It is probably this view which determined General McClellan to wait in expectation about Harper's Ferry. Solicited, in the mean time, by the thousand irresponsible voices of public opinion, as also by the government at Washington, he debouched on the fifteenth of October from Harper's Ferry to the Shenandoah, moved immediately to the left by the mountains, took possession of the defiles which debouch upon Manassas and Centreville, and, advancing prudently, established himself in the environs of Warrenton near the end of October. He found himself in this position the 5th of November, when the Executive power, weary of the delays which it neither understood nor approved, and having, I ought fully to admit, some right to complain of its subordinate, in the matter of a formal obedience to orders, replaced him in his command by General Burnside.

It was not without a certain embarrassment that General Burnside, although he had hitherto well acquitted himself in the command of a corps d'armée, took in hand the direction of the army of fifteen divisions which was unexpectedly confided to him. He, however, did his best to respond to the voice of the government and to the impatience of popular passions. Being aware he had strong masses before him, which obstructed his passage by positions well intrenched upon the upper Rappahannock and its affluents, between Culpepper and Gordonsville, he resolved upon a strategic movement by his left, in order to pass the Rappahannock at Fredericksburg, which had also another advantage, of bringing him near enough to Aquia Creek to make this point one of his bases of operations.

Nothing was more wise than this plan, which may be compared in some respects to that which the Emperor Napoleon III. employed in 1859, in order to cross the Ticino and penetrate into Lombardy. I have already had occasion to say that this movement of the allies, which preceded the battle of Magenta, had not all the desirable celerity, inasmuch as, commenced the 30th of May, Napoleon brought on the field of battle of the 4th of June, hardly the half of the disposable forces. But, such as it was, this movement was executed with giant strides compared with that of Burnside. The Union general threw some troops towards Culpepper on the 15th of November, in order to mask the march of the rest by the left; the 18th his advanced guard arrived at Falmouth, in front of Fredericksburg; and very soon after the remainder of his army, except one division, left in advance of Warrenton, and the corps of occupation of Washington and Alexandria, as a support in the rear.

In order to pass the Rappahannock, bridges were necessary. Of these Burnside had not sufficient. They should have reached him from Washington, but the trains conveying them delayed on the route. It was not till the 10th of December that he was able to put his pontoniers at work, and not till the 13th that he was in readiness to cross the river! For three weeks his movement had been unmasked, and it was hardly necessary for Lee to make a great effort of genius to concentrate himself in good positions in the debouch from Fredericksburg, and to fortify himself there with all ease. Connected with Gordonsville and Richmond by a railroad, he was able even to bring heavy artillery to establish a good intrenched camp, ready to receive the columns of Burnside when they should have gotten through with their troubles of the bridging. In addition to this misfortune, the general in command neglected to feel the enemy, and to throw out a strong reconnoissance upon the right bank, which would have easily shown him the importance of the position of his adversaries. The day of the 13th and the morning of the 14th were, it is true, very cloudy; but this was still more a reason for him to obtain better information. The thing was very capable of being realized. It was dark night, the 17th of June, 1815, when, before Waterloo, Napoleon threw out the cavalry of Milhaud upon the English, to ascertain whether they were simply in bivouac or in position; and there was no need of the *coup d'œil* of a great captain in order to judge, after only five minutes of action, that the adversaries of Milhaud were solidly established and intrenched.

In default of a reconnoissance, Burnside, by reasoning alone, ought to have had more prudence. He had good grounds for expecting, in view of his forced delays, and the little mystery with which his movement had been surrounded, to find before him concentrated masses, which he could not take unawares. In such a state of things he had nothing better to do than to let his movement commence and end there, in order to begin a new one, whether by proceeding on his left or returning by his right, with the hope or conducting it a little more rapidly. But this course he did not judge expedient. It may be from the fact that he was mistaken in the force of the enemy whom he was going to encounter, or that when once his bridges were built he did not dare, from fear of the criticism which would, without doubt, attach itself to his marches and countermarches, to dispense with their use and make a movement to the rear, that he decided on advancing on the 14th. A great battle followed, in which he sustained heavy losses,—about 15,000 men, against a loss of from 3,000 to 4,000 only by the Secessionists. The 16th, Burnside recrossed the Rappahannock without other misadventure, a retreat which, in such circumstances, and against a serious adversary, might have been more disastrous than that of the Berezina, but which, owing to measures extremely well taken, seconded by the inaction of Lee, he effected very successfully.

From that time even to the present, all has been quiet upon this portion of the theatre of the war. The Rappahannock separates the advanced posts of the combatants, which reach, with nearly equal extent, into the region of the mountains

During this time the forces of the West, in Kentucky, in Tennessee, and along the Mississippi, did not remain inactive. Although the operations in these latitudes had been still more irregular than in the East, and though they have had thus far only a secondary importance, I will also say a few words of them.

The opening of the campaign had been fortunate for the arms of the North, and afforded glimpses of brilliant success. Halleck, well seconded by his lieutenants, Pope and Mitchel among others, had retaken complete possession of Kentucky and of Tennessee, and had advanced, with the assistance of the gunboats, even into Alabama and to the frontiers of South Carolina. After him, in the month of August, his successors, Generals Grant, Buell, and Rosecrans had a much more difficult task.

Whilst the Federals, thinking only of gaining ground ahead, offered front on the side of the South and of the West, seeking, on the one hand, to retake the basin of the Mississippi, with the co-operation of the flotilla, and, on the other, to advance into Alabama, bands of rebel guerillas had formed themselves upon their rear, and very soon gravely menaced their communications. These guerillas, grouping themselves little by little, had formed two principal masses: one under the orders of the Generals Stephenson, Armstrong, and Duncan, surrounding Nashville, and seeking to retake the capital of Tennessee from the Federals, who, happily, had solidly intrenched themselves there; another mass, under Generals Bragg and Kirby Smith, reinforced by detachments arrived from Western Virginia, moved into Kentucky against the capital of that State.

A strong party of rebel cavalry, under the orders of General Morgan, hastened with intrepidity between these two corps, and made many fruitful raids upon the Federal detachments.

At the commencement of the month of September, Nashville was very closely besieged by the Secessionists, while Kirby Smith obtained, the 30th of August, over the Federals commanded by General Nelson, a decided victory at Richmond, in Kentucky. This victory opened to Kirby Smith the road to Frankfort, the capital of the State.

General Buell moved to the succor of the Federal forces, already hemmed in, in the north of Kentucky, about the triangle formed by the course of the Ohio, by the Louisville and Lexington railroad, and by the Lexington and Cincinnati railroad.

The terror was great throughout all that country. The government of Kentucky evacuated its capital the 1st of September in order to retire to Louisville. Lexington, Paris, and other neighboring cities, were also abandoned by the Federals, and the Secessionists advanced even in sight of Louisville and of Cincinnati, threatening to cross the river towards these two points, and to invade the States of Indiana and Ohio.

The 16th and 17th of September very sharp engagements took place at Munfordsville, where Bragg captured about four thousand Federals.

But after that, Buell having been able to reach Louisville before Bragg, the Secessionists were obliged to renounce their object, and retreated from the Ohio. They nevertheless maintained a very bold front, and harassed incessantly the Federal flanks by the indefatigable Morgan.

Buell was only able to effect a slow pursuit, of very little advantage. The 8th of October an action took place at Perryville; the 11th, another at Danville, in which Bragg was obliged to retreat, but without suffering himself to be seriously annoyed. He went to reinforce in part the guerillas investing Nashville.

At this moment General Buell was replaced in his command by General Rosecrans, who, during this time, had bravely held in check the Secession Generals Price and Van Dorn, in Mississippi, and had had, among others, a warm and successful affair at Iuka, the 19th of September.

In the first days of November, Rosecrans succeeding in raising the siege of Nashville, and, neglecting the enterprises that Morgan was continuing in Kentucky, he advanced against Bragg, who reunited his various corps while retreating, to the south of Nashville, about the railroad, and very nearly half way from Chattanooga. There General Bragg prepared to give battle, should the pursuit be continued, and to this end he had established himself in an advantageous position, in advance of the city of Murfreesboro', along the little Stone River.

Many weeks of preparations were passed on each side without important acts to record, and it was not

6*

till the 26th of December that the action recommenced. That very day the troops of Rosecrans advanced in the direction of Murfreesboro'. They were about forty-five thousand strong, with one hundred cannon, and divided into three principal corps. Bragg had fifty thousand men. Skirmishes took place during several days, and the 30th, battle was engaged in earnest. The Federals had at first the advantage; but the next day, the 31st, their right, under the command of General McCook, was completely overthrown. It lost, besides, near four thousand prisoners and thirty cannon. Nevertheless, Rosecrans held out, and showed as much firmness as *coup-d'œil*. He threw again his left towards the right, using opportunely his artillery, and, night fortunately coming on, he avoided a defeat, at one time imminent.

The 1st and 2d of January the battle was renewed with fury, and finally declared in favor of the Federals. Bragg beat a retreat, the 4th, upon Tullahoma, without allowing himself to be cut up, and carrying away all his booty. The losses were ten thousand men on each side.

More to the right, other operations had had for object the occupation and the defence of the course of the Mississippi itself. Over all this zone had been seen the combined action of the flotillas and the land forces. Cairo, Columbus, Island No. 10, Memphis, having successively been carried by the Unionists, their efforts were especially directed against the fortress of Vicksburg. This city was attacked at several times by water and by land, but it was defended always with courage and with success; it braves yet, to-day, the assaults of the Federals, who are expecting better success from a canal dug on the west side of the river, and intended to turn off the waters in order to leave the city dry. An army of fifty thousand men, under Generals Grant and McClernand, went to operate against Vicksburg, with the co-operation of a flotilla under Commodore Porter from above, and one under Commodore Farragut, coming from below.

The course of the Lower Mississippi is still occupied by the Secessionists at Port Hudson, thirty leagues above New Orleans. Apart from these points, which obstruct the free navigation of the great river,* its whole course is in the hands of the Federals.

Upon the Atlantic coasts, and upon the sea, the condition of affairs is not notably changed. The Secessionists have had some success as privateers, among others, with a vessel constructed in England—the Alabama. They have also retaken the port of Galveston. But the blockade is still as rigorous as in the beginning, and a recent attempt to break it before Charleston has been so promptly repressed that it only makes more evident the real maritime superiority of the Union.

* The Secessionists have just captured there, two gunboats which had cleared the pass at Vicksburg: the Queen of the West and the Indianola.

The fleet of *Monitors*, of which I have already spoken, is actually at sea, and is expected at an early attack against one of the important points of the coast.

In conclusion, the military situation is at this time the following:

The Army of the Potomac, under the orders of General Hooker, successor to Burnside, is *in échelon* to the right and to the left of Centreville, rendered inactive by the muddy state of the country at this season.

Twenty thousand men, under General Foster, menace Richmond from Newbern, in South Carolina.

An army of fifty thousand men, under General Hunter, landed recently at Port Royal, in South Carolina, apparently destined to cut the communications between Savannah and Charleston, in order to operate, according to the circumstances, upon one of these two capitals of the Secessionists.

At New Orleans, the Army of Louisiana, now commanded by General Banks, who has here replaced the skilful and energetic, but a little harsh, General Butler. This army has just retaken Baton Rouge, the capital of Louisiana, and ought to furnish a corps for the borders of Texas, and another to co-operate with the fleet in the capture of Port Hudson and of Vicksburg.

The Army of the Cumberland, or of Tennessee, under the orders of General Rosecrans, operating to the south of Nashville, disposed in a manner to be able, according to the necessity, to co-operate in taking the banks of the Mississippi, or to throw itself by its left upon the Carolinas, so as to join itself to Foster or to Hunter.

Finally, the army of Grant, besieging Vicksburg, and intending, as rapidly as its success will permit, to descend the river and approach Banks, in order, at last, to effect its junction with the latter.

Besides, also, a great number of detached corps, more or less regular, comprising those of the extreme West, in the States of Missouri and Arkansas.

In front of each of these armies the South has also a principal one, under the command of generals already known, that is to say: against Hooker, General Lee; at Charleston, General Beauregard; in the extreme South, Magruder; in Tennessee, Longstreet, having replaced Bragg; at Vicksburg, Van Dorn and Price; and numberless guerilla parties again forming themselves in Tennessee and in Kentucky, upon the rear of Rosecrans and of Grant.

If we compare the actual situation to that of a year ago, we see that the North has made incontestable progress, and that, continuing at this rate, it will arrive, before two or three years, at the end of its principal task. Without doubt, the success has not corresponded to the hopes which the first attempts had excited. The resistance, so obstinate and even brilliant, of the Secessionists in Virginia; their bold designs in Maryland, in Pennsylvania, and at the very doors of Ohio and Indiana, constituted a sensible moral check for the Union, which had for a moment hoped, not without some appearance of reason, to be able to finish the campaign in the course of 1862, and to treat in the autumn, and at Richmond itself, for a durable peace. But this check to its self-love once admitted, the advantage of the arms of the North is incontestable. The success is dearly purchased, it is true, in every way, but it is not less palpable; the North makes five steps in advance, perhaps, and retires three; but there still remain two of advantage.

Having infinitely more resources than the South, it is to be believed, I repeat it, and to be hoped, that in this proportion of sacrifices the Union will triumph, and will be finally restored by the force of arms.

We should be able not to limit ourselves to the hope, but to predict with certainty such a result, were the North more united than it is; were the real sentiment of its situation, as well as that of its historic responsibility, in face of the consequences of the actual crisis, able to overcome, for some time, the deplorable passions of party spirit and of clique; or if, in default of this, the Government could assume strength enough to annihilate the miserable intrigues which daily hinder the conduct of the war. Alas! far from having the power to break the fetters on the military operations, the government itself has not, sometimes, the energy to resist certain currents, springing from the very nature of its republican organization, which cause it to thwart the better measures of the generals. Let us recognize, also, the fact that its task is one of the most arduous : for it is upon it that the fury excited by the disappointments and the accidents necessarily incident to war always discharges itself. While some successes easily raise it in the eyes of the masses, which are in the United States the true sovereign, the reverse which misfortune sends it, or the gradual progress to which it is reduced, creates for it numerous adversaries. The latter give vent to their dissatisfaction in the frequent elections, which proceed regularly during war as in peace, and the official positions in the different States are soon occupied by enemies, more or less ardent, of the Government, who add new complications and new causes of disorder to those of which there were already so many to complain. It is thus that, in several States, as New York, Pennsylvania, and Illinois, recent elections have brought into power declared enemies of the administration of Mr. Lincoln.

Important decisions, however, and which ought to advance the crisis towards a solution, have been made by the President and by Congress. In the beginning of the war, the North, who believed herself stronger than she really is, had for her principal aim the restoration of the Union at every cost. In order to do that, she sought as much as possible to continue in the legal condition, without touching upon the irritating question of slavery, and to accompany her military movements with every desirable restraint. The residents in sympathy with the enemy, although showing themselves profoundly hostile and disdainful, were treated with a mildness and tenderness which bordered upon the ridiculous. The smallest supplies furnished by them were paid for at an excessively high rate, and in ready money, while everywhere else, in Europe, requisitions would have been made upon them. Their blacks, amongst other things, were as much respected as the most sacred relics. And these measures, I repeat it, were dictated by the thought that, after some military successes which they should easily obtain, the ambitious leaders of the South would be discarded, and that peace would be made upon the same basis of the old Constitution of the Union, guaranteeing to the States of the South their slave property. Perhaps some advantage would be taken of the circumstance, to establish some conditions in favor of slow and gradual emancipation, but on this point there was no certainty.

The reverses of the Federals, in the course of the summer, introduced other reflections and other sentiments. The North ought to have perceived, to the detriment of her vanity, that she was not in a state to treat the South in a forbearing manner, and that all her means would not be too much to enable her to carry on the contest with advantage. But in the

South, while the whites fought, the negro slaves cultivated the soil, looked after the farms, produced, in a word, the resources which served to support the war. Sometimes, even, they employed them as laborers in the works of fortification. To guarantee to the South, from pure scruples for the right of the Constitution, such a facility, became the excess of good-nature. As much would it have availed to guarantee her gunpowder, under the pretext that it is black.

On the other side, a party very noisy, and become, as all extreme parties do, more and more powerful in the proportion of the reverses, by the very logic of its situation—the abolition party—lost no occasion to demand imperiously the immediate emancipation of the slaves. Her journals, her orators, the eloquent Senator Sumner among others, caused persuasive words to resound through the land.

Under this double influence, the Federal government, which had already decreed many partial acts of confiscation of the slaves of the rebels in arms, and a bill in favor of gradual emancipation, with indemnity to the proprietors, and plans of colonization, had no trouble in deciding to strike the grand blow. The 22d of September, President Lincoln issued a proclamation, in which he announced, as a war measure, that all the slaves of the proprietors in arms against the Union, on the 1st day of January, 1863, should be in fact free, and that the civil and military officers of the United States should render them assistance. This great resolution, sanctioned by Congress, was afterwards put in execution, as far as it was possible, by a second proclamation of President Lincoln, on the 1st January, 1863, declaring free the slaves of all the States and portions of States still at war against the Union. It was followed by another bill, dated the 16th of February, 1863, ordering the arming of the blacks, and their formation into regiments, which bill was immediately put in execution. At all the points of the Slave States where the Federals have succeeded in gaining a foot-hold, special recruiting offices for the negroes have been opened, and at this time eighty regiments of blacks are in formation. Not only have the blacks aided in supporting the vitality of the South by their labors, but they will second the military action of the North, and by that means the latter has certainly acquired a double advantage.

In return, it has excited a redundancy of rage in the Secession States, of which the President, Mr. Jefferson Davis, has allowed himself to proceed, by a proclamation, to menaces of cruel reprisals, which, it is hoped, will remain without application. In the North, under the flag of which march, it is known, several Slave States, the act of emancipation has created also numerous malcontents. The party called Democratic has made of it an electoral arm, and is now still using it with skill and with success to destroy the influence of the Republican party and the power of the President.

Whatever may be the result of these secondary struggles, breaking out in the midst of the torrent of the gigantic contest of the North against the South, the fact and the right of the emancipation proclaimed will remain intact for those whom it has been able to reach. The cause of the equality of the races will have been equally advanced by the organization of the black regiments, which will be a fortunate precedent, and, in these two respects, the friends of Christian equality ought to hail with pleasure the acts of Mr. Lincoln, even though they have been brought about incidentally, and qualified as measures of war rather than as acts of justice.

A bill instituting the conscription for the levies which would be necessary in the future, and adopted in the course of February by Congress, completes the series of salutary measures with which the events have inspired the administration. By means of an army recruited by conscription, and provided with officers who can be chosen outside of miserable political influences, the reign of law can be more easily assured against the attempts to support rather than oppose, even in the very North itself, the work of secession.

In conclusion, I will mention here some of the principal sources from which can be derived information upon the events more particularly military.

The *journals* and *reviews*, so numerous in the United States, are to be consulted in the front rank, for all give detailed news of the operations. This examination, however, requires some sagacity, as well as knowledge of the manner in which military affairs are conducted in general, and in the United States in particular, where politics and a thousand personal intrigues are continual. These journals are ordinarily of large size. They abound in correspondence from the camps, which occupies many columns, and often contains very contradictory information. To read, only, and to examine these primitive elements of history in the papers, ordinarily badly printed and in very small type, afterwards to compare and weigh the facts received, in order to arrive at the truth, constitute a toil of great length, and often discouraging.

The *official reports* of the generals are seldom printed, except by the care of the government, which often abridges them,—a course fully justifiable in the face of the enemy,—of the most striking passages. These reports are ordinarily very long, diffuse, entangled, interspersed with phrases according to the need of particular occasions. One would take them often for diplomatic notes, for the mandates of an attorney, or for polemic articles, as much as for reports really military. In the simple reading of these diverse official accounts, one can see how much the service of the staff is under-estimated in the army. Some, however, of Generals Halleck, McClellan, and Butler, among others, can be noticed as honorable exceptions among the great number.

The procès verbaux of the courts-martial and of the courts of inquiry constitute an element of publicity, and of historical sources, peculiar to the United States, and of the highest value. I have already spoken of the institution of these innumerable courts of justice, where the generals and the highest functionaries of the government come to make their depositions, and to be submitted to interrogatories like simple witnesses in a court of correction. If this machinery complicates sometimes the operations and gravely disturbs the discipline, it is necessary, in return, to recognize the fact that it signally facilitates the task of history, and in this respect I should be the last to complain of it. By the free practice of these courts, almost all the important operations pass through the sieve of public inquiry and of contradictory discussion. Those of Generals Smith, McDowell, Porter, Pope, Frémont, Burnside, Buell, &c., and the *procès-verbaux* which have resulted from them, furnish documents of the greatest value for the understanding of the movements in which these generals have participated; but they demand, on account of their prolixity, a great allowance of patience on the part of persons desirous of deriving profit from them.

The annual reports of administration of the ministers, to the President and to Congress, are also documents of high value, which have the particular merit of being more explicit and less extended than the preceding. They demand, however, some reserve of confidence, seeing that they are prepared particularly with a view to justify the administration. It is necessary to complete them by the observations made in the chambers and in the different committees, among others, in the military committee of the Senate.

The various *annual almanacs* have the custom of publishing a chronological sketch of the military events, where one can easily find certain dates or proper names. But we ought to avoid their figures as much as reflections, and to know how to rectify them by taking into the account the political complexion of the editor.

An interesting publication, and which would be still more so if it did not threaten to become too voluminous, is edited in New York, and has for its title: *Rebellion Record*. It has already reached its twenty-fourth volume, and will probably have, in the same proportion, a sixtieth in order to arrive at the actual period of the war. It comprises three parts: one, much the most important, comprising official and semi-official documents; another containing a collection of divers incidents in the campaign, and which has the pretension, a little exaggerated, of being a journal of the operations; the third, a medley of poetry, songs, anecdotes, and of occasional editorial remarks.

A great number of *pamphlets*, controversial or biographical, have also been published in various cities of the United States. Two among others, of Colonel Ellet, Engineer, who organized the ram flotillas of the Mississippi; two of General Frémont, on the subject of his different commands; one upon General McClellan; many upon the capture of New Orleans, &c., are instructive. It is not within my knowledge that there have appeared, thus far, books of some value, treating specially of the military events in an historical point of view. A volume: *The War in America*, by the Kentuckian, Colonel Schafner, edited at London, treats only of the political part. The same is true of another by Count Gurowski. There is one announced by the General of Engineers, *Barnard*, which ought to be more instructive. There is some information offered in regard to the South, in a little book which has just appeared in French, at Geneva, and entitled: *Treize Mois dans l'Armée des Rebelles*.[*]

Many literary men have already undertaken vast publications, and, very recently, one of them has commenced by sending a circular to all the generals, to announce to them his enterprise, and desiring them at the same time to fill up a formula to contain the extent of their civil and military services, and the detail of their exploits. There will consequently be no

---

[*] Thirteen Months in the Army of the Rebels. Adventures of a Volunteer Enlisted in spite of Himself, by William G. Stevenson, of New York. 1 vol. 12mo. Geneva, press of Ramboz & Schuchart.

want of light on the subject of this campaign, especially on the side of the North. But, of all these sources, the most valuable will be, without doubt, the publications which, according to custom, will be ordered by the Senate, joined to the commentaries of the several commanding generals.

In Europe, England has furnished, besides a great number of writings upon slavery, some books upon the events in the United States, but all treating of the political rather than of the military part. From the *Diary North and South* of Mr. Russell, correspondent of the *Times*, and from various letters addressed to that journal, one can, however, draw interesting military information. It is necessary, however, to notice the political disfavor which the cause of the Union finds among the English, and not to admit the humorsome appreciations of their writers, otherwise than on the condition of not being obliged to believe them.

In Germany, the daily journals, the *Allgemeine Zeitung* among others, have received, more than once, excellent communications upon the war of the United States. A number of the papers have reproduced, among others, the impressions of a Prussian officer, an actor in the ranks of the South, which deserve to be noticed. We are able to learn from this officer that in the campaign of the peninsula of Yorktown, there was great disorder in the midst of the Secession army after the battle of Fair Oaks, and that if McClellan had had only some thousand men more, so as to advance, he would undoubtedly have entered Richmond.

A book, favorably announced, has appeared at Frankfort, at the end of 1861, going back even to the opening of the campaign. The author, Mr. Aneke, analyzes very well all the preliminaries of the struggle. He belongs to the extreme Republican party, and should take service under the United States as an artillery officer. If this work is finished, it will not fail, to judge by what is already known of it, to offer a genuine interest to the public.

In France there have been published two works, particularly worthy of mention.

In the first place, *Lettres sur l'Amérique*, by M. Lieutenant-Colonel Ferri Pisani, aide-de-camp of Prince Napoleon, who made, in 1861, a visit to the two belligerent camps. These piquant letters, of an officer as intelligent as experienced, form on the whole a very faithful picture, though sometimes a little too imaginative, of the military movements which the author has had under his eyes. They give little historical detail, but they have an originality of perception and of comparison, a delicacy of glance, and a charm of style, which make it to be much regretted that they were not continued even to the period of the important events which followed. They have, again, been the first to furnish to Europe some little information, characteristic and precise, upon the transatlantic troubles. On this occasion, begging you, *Mr. Coun-*

7

sellor, to excuse my speaking again of myself, I can well avow that it was the perusal of these letters in the *Moniteur de l'Armée*, in October, 1861, which determined me to make also a military excursion in America; and, in spite of some slurs, a little sarcastic, flung at the Yankees by the witty French officer, I have but to thank him to-day for having contributed to give me a more ample acquaintance with the country.

Another French book, elegantly drawn from notes of an eye-witness, constitutes one of the most remarkable publications upon this war. It is a small volume entitled: *Campagne de l'Armée du Potomac*, and published at first in the *Revue des Deux-Mondes*. They attribute it to the Prince de Joinville, and with reason, I think. The Prince de Joinville constantly accompanied the staff of General McClellan, where figured, as captains and aides-de-camp, his two nephews, the Count de Paris and the Duke de Chartres. He was then well situated to take note of the events, and each evening, in the bivouac as under the tent, his note-book received precious deposits for history. Joining to this advantage a great experience, and sound principles in the matter of military operations, a correct and elevated judgment, and a quite peculiar talent of observation, the author has been able to give to this book, which it will not be necessary to judge upon its size, the stamp of an excellent work. It is one of the first sources upon which we ought to draw, in order to possess a just idea of what is actually taking place in the United States. It brings the reader down to the end of the campaign of the Peninsula of Yorktown—a campaign which comprises considerable military feats, also the famous battle of the Seven Days, upon the Chickahominy and the James River, of which the account is given with the greatest perspicuity. It is to be hoped that the eminent author will not rest there, and that, among others, he will assure the public of his estimation of the novel marine of the United States—a subject at present so important, and which few persons in Europe would be able to approach with the same authority as himself.

I have yet to mention, among the French publications, the *Ephémérides* of the *Moniteur de l'Armée*, compiled generally with care and impartiality. They have the same kind of usefulness as the American almanacs, and would surpass them in merit if they did not include sufficiently numerous errors, geographical and others.

The *Moniteur Universel* contains also, once or twice a week, American correspondence, of which some furnish useful military information, and all denote a solid knowledge of the country, joined, unfortunately, to a severity, often excessive, on the side of the cause of the Union. Two other papers of Paris, the *Siècle*, and especially the *Journal des Débats*, sustain on the other hand, with zeal and talent, the principles for which the Federals make so many sacrifices. The *Journal des Débats* has always given, by the side of good, substantial articles, more of details than its colleagues upon this struggle.

Among the occasional political publications, the *République Américaine* of M. Xavier Eyma, an ardent volume of M. the Count of Gasparin, *Un Grand Peuple qui se relève*, and divers articles of the *Revue Chrétienne*, among others, of M. the minister Fisch,* ought not to be neglected.

In Switzerland, it is in the columns of the *Journal de Genève*, in its important correspondence from New York, among others, that we find the best opinions upon the events in the United States.

I conclude here, Mr. Federal Counsellor, the supplements which I thought ought to follow my report of the 9th of August, 1862, and, while thanking you anew for the kindness with which you have deigned to accept it, I have the honor to reiterate to you the assurance of my most respectful devotion.

Fd. Lecomte,
Federal Lieutenant-Colonel.

Lausanne, *March* 16th, 1863.

* The articles of M. Fisch have been collected in one volume: Etats-Unis en 1861. 1 vol. 12mo. Paris, 1861.

D. Van Nostrand's Publications.

Evolutions of Field Batteries of Artillery.

Translated from the French, and arranged for the Army and Militia of the United States. By Gen. ROBERT ANDERSON, U. S. Army. Published by order of the War Department. 1 vol. cloth, 32 plates. $1.

WAR DEPARTMENT, *Nov.* 2d, 1859.

The System of "Evolutions of Field Batteries," translated from the French, and arranged for the service of the United States, by Major Robert Anderson, of the 1st Regiment of Artillery, having been approved by the President, is published for the information and government of the army.

All Evolutions of Field Batteries not embraced in this system are prohibited, and those herein prescribed will be strictly observed.

J. B. FLOYD, *Secretary of War.*

"This system having been adopted by the War Department, is to the artillerist what Hardee's Tactics is to the infantry soldier; the want of a work like this has been seriously felt, and will be eagerly welcomed."—*Louisville Journal.*

Standing Orders of the Seventh Regiment, National Guard.

For the Regulation and Government of the Regiment in the Field or in Quarters. By A. DURYEE, Colonel. New edition, flexible cloth. 40 cents.

"This, which is a new edition of a popular work, cannot fail to be eagerly sought after, as presenting clearly and succinctly the principles of organization and discipline of a most favorite corps. An appropriate index facilitates reference to the matter of the volume."—*New Yorker.*

Light Infantry Company and Skirmish Drill.

The Company Drill of the Infantry of the Line, together with the Skirmish Drill of the Company and Battalion, after the Method of General LE LOUTEREL. Bayonet Fencing; with a Supplement on the Handling and Service of Light Infantry. By J. MUNROE, Col. 22d Regiment, N. G., N. Y. S. M., formerly Capt. U. S Infantry. 1 vol., 32mo.

D. Van Nostrand's Publications.

Siege of Bomarfund (1854).

Journals of Operations of the Artillery and Engineers. Published by permission of the Minister of War. Illustrated by maps and plans. Translated from the French by an Army Officer. 1 vol. 12mo, cloth. 75 cents.

"To military men this little volume is of special interest. It contains a translation by an officer of the United States Army, of the journal of operations by the artillery and engineers at the siege of Bomarsund in 1854, published by permission of the French Minister of War in the *Journal des Armées speciales et de l'Etat Major*. The account of the same successful attack, given by Sir Howard Douglas in the new edition of his work on Gunnery, is appended; and the narrative is illustrated by elaborate maps and plans."—*New York Paper*.

Lefsons and Practical Notes on Steam,

The Steam-Engine, Propellers, &c., &c., for Young Marine Engineers, Students, and others. By the late W. R. KING, U. S. N. Revised by Chief-Engineer J. W. KING, U. S. Navy. Sixth edition, enlarged. 8vo, cloth. $2.00

"This is the second edition of a valuable work of the late W. R. KING, U. S. N. It contains lessons and practical notes on Steam and the Steam-Engine, Propellers, &c. It is calculated to be of great use to young marine engineers, students, and others. The text is illustrated and explained by numerous diagrams and representations of machinery. This new edition has been revised and enlarged by Chief Engineer J. W. KING, U. S. N., brother to the deceased author of the work."—*Boston Daily Advertiser.*

"This is one of the best, because eminently plain and practical, treatises on the Steam-Engine ever published."—*Philadelphia Press.*

"Its re-publication at this time, when so many young men are entering the service as naval engineers, is most opportune. Each of them ought to have a copy."—*Philadelphia Evening Bulletin.*

Manual of Internal Rules and Regulations for Men-of-War.

By Commodore U. P. LEVY, U. S. N., late Flag-officer commanding U. S. Naval Force in the Mediterranean, &c. Flexible blue cloth. Second edition, revised and enlarged. 50 cents.

"Among the professional publications for which we are indebted to the war, we willingly give a prominent place to this useful little Manual of Rules and Regulations to be observed on board of ships of war. Its authorship is a sufficient guarantee for its accuracy and practical value; and as a guide to young officers in providing for the discipline, police, and sanitary government of the vessels under their command, we know of nothing superior."—*N. Y. Herald.*

"Should be in the hands of every Naval officer, of whatever grade, and will not come amiss to any intelligent mariner."—*Boston Traveller.*

"A work which will prove of great utility, in both the Naval service and the mercantile marine."—*Baltimore American.*

D. Van Nostrand's Publications.

Hand-Book of Artillery,

For the Service of the United States Army and Militia. New and revised edition. By Maj. JOSEPH ROBERTS, U. S. A. 1 vol. 18mo, cloth. $1.

"A complete catechism of gun practice, covering the whole ground of this branch of military science, and adapted to militia and volunteer drill, as well as to the regular army. It has the merit of precise detail, even to the technical names of all parts of a gun, and how the smallest operations connected with its use can be best performed. It has evidently been prepared with great care, and with strict scientific accuracy. By the recommendation of a committee appointed by the commanding officer of the Artillery School at Fort Monroe, Va., it has been substituted for 'Burns' Questions and Answers,' an English work which has heretofore been the text-book of instruction in this country."
—*New York Century.*

New Infantry Tactics,

For the Instruction, Exercise, and Manœuvres of the Soldier, a Company, Line of Skirmishers, Battalion, Brigade, or Corps d'Armée. By Brig.-Gen. SILAS CASEY, U. S. A. 3 vols. 24mo. Half roan, lithographed plates. $2.50.

VOL. I.—School of the Soldier; School of the Company; Instruction for Skirmishers.

VOL. II.—School of the Battalion.

VOL. III.—Evolutions of a Brigade; Evolutions of a Corps d'Armée.

"The manuscript of this new system of Infantry Tactics was carefully examined by General McCLELLAN, and met with his unqualified approval, which he has since manifested by authorizing General CASEY to adopt it for his entire division. The author has retained much that is valuable contained in the systems of SCOTT and HARDEE, but has made many important changes and additions which experience and the exigencies of the service require. General CASEY'S reputation as an accomplished soldier and skilful tactician is a guarantee that the work he has undertaken has been thoroughly performed.

"These volumes are based on the French *ordonnances* of 1831 and 1845 for the manœuvres of heavy infantry and *chasseurs à pied;* both of these systems have been in use in our service for some years, the former having been translated by Gen. Scott, and the latter by Col. Hardee. After the introduction of the latter drill in our service, in connection with Gen. Scott's Tactics, there arose the necessity of a uniform system for the manœuvres of all the infantry arm of the service. These volumes are the result of the author's endeavor to communicate the instruction, now used and adopted in the army, to achieve this result."—*Boston Journal.*

"Based on the best precedents, adapted to the novel requirements of the art of war, and very full in its instructions, Casey's Tactics will be received as the most useful and most comprehensive work of its kind in our language. From the drill and discipline of the individual soldier, or through all the various combinations, to the manœuvres of a brigade and the evolutions of a Corps D'Armée, the student is advanced by a clear method and steady progress. Numerous cuts, plans, and diagrams illustrate positions and movements, and demonstrate to the eye the exact working out of the individual position, brigading, order of battle, &c., &c. The work is a model of publishing success, being in three neat pocket volumes."—*New Yorker.*

Sword-Play.

THE MILITIAMAN'S MANUAL AND SWORD-PLAY WITHOUT A MASTER.—Rapier and Broad-Sword Exercises copiously Explained and Illustrated; Small-Arm Light Infantry Drill of the United States Army; Infantry Manual of Percussion Muskets; Company Drill of the United States Cavalry. By Major M. W. BERRIMAN, engaged for the last thirty years in the practical instruction of Military Students. Second edition. 1 vol. 12mo, red cloth. $1.

"Captain Berriman has had thirty years' experience in teaching military students, and his work is written in a simple, clear, and soldierly style. It is illustrated with twelve plates, and is one of the cheapest and most complete works of the kind published in this country."—*New York World.*

"This work will be found very valuable to all persons seeking military instruction; but it recommends itself most especially to officers, and those who have to use the sword or sabre. We believe it is the only work on the use of the sword published in this country."—*New York Tablet.*

"It is a work of obvious merit and value."—*Boston Traveller.*

Official Army Regifter for 1863.

New edition. 8vo, paper. 50 cents.

The Artillerift's Manual:

Compiled from various Sources, and adapted to the Service of the United States. Profusely illustrated with woodcuts and engravings on stone. Second edition, revised and corrected, with valuable additions. By Capt. JOHN GIBBON, U. S. Army. 1 vol. 8vo, half roan, $5.

This book is now considered the standard authority for that particular branch of the Service in the United States Army. The War Department, at Washington, has exhibited its thorough appreciation of the merits of this volume, the want of which has been hitherto much felt in the service, by subscribing for 700 copies.

"It is with great pleasure that we welcome the appearance of a new work on this subject, entitled 'The Artillerist's Manual,' by Capt. John Gibbon, a highly scientific and meritorious officer of artillery in our regular service. The work, an octavo volume of 500 pages, in large, clear type, appears to be well adapted to supply just what has been heretofore needed to fill the gap between the simple Manual and the more abstruse demonstrations of the science of gunnery. The whole work is profusely illustrated with woodcuts and engravings on stone, tending to give a more complete and exact idea of the various matters described in the text. The book may well be considered as a valuable and important addition to the military science of the country."—*New York Herald.*

D. Van Nostrand's Publications.

The Political and Military History of the Campaign of Waterloo.

Translated from the French of General BARON DE JOMINI. By Capt. S. V. BENET, U. S. Ordnance. 1 vol. 12mo, cloth, second edition. 75 cents.

"Baron Jomini has the reputation of being one of the greatest military historians and critics of the century. His merits have been recognized by the highest military authorities in Europe, and were rewarded in a conspicuous manner by the greatest military power in Christendom. He learned the art of war in the school of experience, the best and only finishing school of the soldier. He served with distinction in nearly all the campaigns of Napoleon, and it was mainly from the gigantic military operations of this matchless master of the art that he was enabled to discover its true principles, and to ascertain the best means of their application in the infinity of combinations which actual war presents. Jomini criticizes the details of Waterloo with great science, and yet in a manner that interests the general reader as well as the professional."—*New York World.*

"This book by Jomini, though forming the twenty-second chapter of his 'Life of Napoleon,' is really a unit in itself, and forms a complete summary of the campaign. It is an interesting volume, and deserves a place in the affections of all who would be accomplished military men."—*New York Times.*

"The present volume is the concluding portion of his great work, 'Vie Politique et Militaire de Napoleon,' published in 1826. Capt. Benet's translation of it has been for some time before the public, and has now reached a second edition; it is very ably executed, and forms a work which will always be interesting, and especially so at a time when military affairs are uppermost in the public mind."—*Philadelphia North American.*

The "C. S. A." and the Battle of Bull Run.

(A Letter to an English friend), by J. G. BARNARD, Major of Engineers, U. S. A., Brigadier-General and Chief Engineer, Army of the Potomac. With five maps. 1 vol., 8vo., cloth. $1.50.

"This book was begun by the author as a letter to a friend in England, but as he proceeded and his MSS. increased in magnitude, he changed his original plan, and the book is the result. General Barnard gives by far the best, most comprehensible and complete account of the Battle of Bull Run we have seen. It is illustrated by some beautifully drawn maps, prepared for the War Department by the topographical engineers. He demonstrates to a certainty that but for the causeless panic the day might not have been lost. The author writes with vigor and earnestness, and has contributed one of the most valuable records yet published of the history of the war."—*Boston Commercial Bulletin.*

"A spirited and reliable view of the true character of the secession movement, and a correct account of the Battle of Bull Run, by a military man whose qualifications for the task are equalled but by few persons."—*Cincinnati Gazette.*

"The work is clearly written, and can but leave the impression upon every reader's mind that it is truth. We commend it to the perusal of every one who wants an intelligent, truthful and graphic description of the 'C. S. A.,' and the Battle of Bull Run."—*New York Observer.*

D. Van Nostrand's Publications.

Maxims and Instructions on the Art of War.

Maxims, Advice, and Instructions on the Art of War; or, A Practical Military Guide for the use of Soldiers of all Arms and of all Countries. Translated from the French, by Captain LENDY, Director of the Practical Military College, late of the French Staff, etc., etc. 1 vol., 18mo., cloth. 75 cents.

"A book of maxims, that is not as dry as a cask of 'remainder biscuit,' is a novelty in literature. The little volume before us is an exception to the general rule. It presents the suggestion of common sense in military affairs, with a certain brilliancy and point. One may read it purely for entertainment, and not be disappointed. At the same time, it is full of practical instructions of great value. When found in the pocket of an officer of volunteers, it will be the right book in the right place."—*N. Y. Tribune.*

"We do not pretend to much military science, but we have found this small volume easy to understand and interesting to read. It is compiled from old works, but is adapted to new notions and improvements, and it gives in a nutshell a general idea of the whole business of war. Some men who have always maintained 'Quaker' principles, and who have never studied the trade and mystery of fighting, find it difficult to comprehend the various strategic movements that are chronicled from day to day in the newspapers. These men should look into the subject of war, and we advise them, as a beginning, to read this book. It will probably help their cloudy perceptions, and enable them to see clearly the meaning of military operations, which now they cannot understand."—*Providence Journal.*

Nolan's System for Training Cavalry Horses.

By KENNER GARRARD, Captain Fifth Cavalry, U. S. A. 1 vol., 12mo, cloth. 24 Lithographed plates. $1.50.

* * * "We are glad when competent men bring forward works that are intended to facilitate the formation of an effective cavalry force. Of this class is *Nolan's System for Training Cavalry Horses*, prepared for use in this country, by Captain Kenner Garrard, U. S. A. Captain Nolan was distinguished in the British service for his knowledge of the cavalry arm, and for his general talents. As the work had become out of print, Captain Garrard has done well in reproducing it; he has added to it a chapter on Rarey's Method of Training Horses, and another on Horse Shoeing. The volume is well illustrated. It cannot be too warmly commended to general use."—*Boston Daily Evening Traveller.*

"It explains a perfectly successful method of gaining the mastery over the most refractory horse, and is no less adapted for the use of the rider for exercise, business, or pleasure than of the cavalry officer. By the plan of the author, the time of training is greatly shortened; the progress is so gradual that it never makes the horse unamiable, and the successive lessons tend to the development of mutual love and admiration between the parties."—*N. Y. Tribune.*

D. Van Nostrand's Publications.

School of the Guides.

Designed for the use of the Militia of the United States. Flexible cloth. 50 cents.

"This excellent compilation condenses into a compass of less than sixty pages all the instruction necessary for the guides, and the information being disconnected with other matters, is more readily referred to and more easily acquired."—*Louisville Journal.*

"The work is carefully got up, and is illustrated by numerous figures, which make the positions of the guides plain to the commonest understanding. Those of our sergeants who wish to be 'posted' in their duties should procure a copy."—*Sunday Mercury, Philadelphia.*

"It has received high praise, and will prove of great service in perfecting the drill of our Militia."—*N. American and U. S. Gazette, Phil.*

"This neat hand-book of the elementary movements on which the art of the tactician is based, reflects great credit on Col. LE GAL, whose reputation is deservedly high among military men. No soldier should be without the School of the Guides."—*New York Daily News.*

Gunnery in 1858:

A Treatise on Rifles, Cannon, and Sporting Arms. By WM. GREENER, C. E. 1 vol. 8vo, cloth. $3.

Manual of Heavy Artillery.

For the Use of Volunteers. 1 vol. 12mo. Red cloth. 75 cents.

"Should be in the hands of every Artillerist."—*N. Y. Illustrated News.*

"This is a concise and well-prepared Manual, adapted to the wants of Volunteers. The instruction, which is of an important nature, is presented in a simple and clear style, such as will be easily understood. The volume is also illustrated with explanatory cuts and drawings. It is a work of practical value, and one needed at the present time in the service."—*Boston Commercial Bulletin.*

"An indispensable Manual for all who wish easily and accurately to learn the school of the Artillerist."—*N. Y. Commercial Advertiser.*

Auftrian Infantry Tactics.

Evolutions of the Line as practised by the Austrian Infantry, and adopted in 1853. Translated by Capt. C. M. WILCOX, Seventh Regiment U. S. Infantry. 1 vol. 12mo. Three large plates, cloth. $1.

"The movements of armies engaged in battle have often been compared to those of the chess-board, and we cannot doubt that there are certain principles of tactics in actual war as in that game, which may determine the result independently, in a great measure, of the personal strength and courage of the men engaged. The difference between these principles as applied in the American Army and in the Austrian, is so wide as to have suggested the translation of the work before us, which contains the whole result of the famous Field-Marshal RADETZKY'S experience for twenty-five years, while in supreme command in Italy."—*New York Century.*

D. Van Nostrand's Publications.

Naval Light Artillery.

Instruction for Naval Light Artillery, afloat and ashore, prepared and arranged for the U. S. Naval Academy, by Lieut. W. H. PARKER, U. S. N. Second edition, revised by Lieut. S. B. LUCE, U. S. N., Assistant Instructor of Gunnery and Tactics at the United States Naval Academy. 1 vol., 8vo., cloth, with 22 plates, $1.50.

"The service for which this is the text-book of instruction is of special importance in the present war. The use of light boat-pieces is constant and important, and young officers are frequently obliged to leave their boats, take their pieces ashore, and manœuvre them as field artillery. Not unfrequently, also, they are incorporated, when ashore, with troops, and must handle their guns like the artillery soldiers of a battery. 'The Exercise of the Howitzer Afloat' was prepared and arranged by Captain Dahlgren, whose name gives additional sanction and value to the book. A Manual for the Sword and Pistol is also given. The plates are numerous and exceedingly clear, and the whole typography excellent."
Philadelphia Inquirer.

New Manual of Sword and Sabre Exercife.

By Colonel J. C. KELTON, U. S. A. Thirty plates. *In Press.*

History of the United States Naval Academy,

With Biographical Sketches, and the names of all the Superintendents, Professors and Graduates, to which is added a Record of some of the earliest Votes by Congress, of Thanks, Medals, and Swords to Naval Officers. By EDWARD CHAUNCEY MARSHALL, A. M. 1 vol., 12mo., cloth, plates. $1.

"The book before us affords a good account of the naval school from its first establishment under the auspices of Secretary Bancroft, with full statements of the regulations, requisites for admission, course of study, etc. It is a seasonable and useful contribution to the history of education in this country."—*N. Y. Independent.*

"This is a most welcome volume. All that throws light on the history of our army and navy now needs study, and the Naval Academy, though really so recent, well deserves a history. Mr. Marshall has depicted, in clear and graphic language, the vain struggle for years to give our navy, what the navy of every nation has, an academy to form the young officers for their important duties."—*N. Y. Historical Magazine.*

"Every naval man will find it not only a pleasant companion, but an invaluable book of reference. It is seldom that so much information is made accessible in so agreeable a manner in so small a space."—*New York Times.*

D. Van Nostrand's Publications.

A Treatife on Ordnance and Naval Gunnery.

Compiled and arranged as a Text-Book for the U. S. Naval Academy, by Lieutenant EDWARD SIMPSON, U. S. N. Second edition, revised and enlarged. 1 vol. 8vo, plates and cuts, half morocco. $4.

"As the compiler has charge of the instruction in Naval Gunnery at the Naval Academy, his work, in the compilation of which he has consulted a large number of eminent authorities, is probably well suited for the purpose designed by it—namely, the circulation of information which many officers, owing to constant service afloat, may not have been able to collect. In simple and plain language it gives instruction as to cannon, gun carriages, gun powder, projectiles, fuzes, locks, and primers; the theory of pointing guns, rifles, the practice of gunnery, and a great variety of other similar matters, interesting to fighting men on sea and land."—*Washington Daily Globe.*

"A vast amount of information is conveyed in a readable and familiar form. The illustrations are excellent, and many of them unique, being colored or bronzed so as to represent various military arms, &c., with more than photographic literalness."—*Washington Star.*

"It is scarcely necessary for us to say that a work prepared by a writer so practically conversant with all the subjects of which he treats, and who has such a reputation for scientific ability, cannot fail to take at once a high place among the text-books of our naval service. It has been approved by the Secretary of the Navy, and will henceforth be one of the standard authorities on all matters connected with Naval Gunnery."—*New York Herald.*

"The book itself is admirably arranged, characterized by great simplicity and clearness, and certainly at this time will be a most valuable one to officers of the Navy."—*Boston Commercial Bulletin.*

"Originally designed as a text-book, it is now enlarged, and so far modified in its plan as to make it an invaluable hand-book for the naval officer. It is comprehensive—preserving the cream of many of the best books on ordnance and naval gunnery, and is printed and illustrated in the most admirable manner."—*New York World.*

Elementary Inftruction in Naval Ordnance and Gunnery.

By JAMES H. WARD, Commander U. S. Navy, Author of "Naval Tactics," and "Steam for the Million." New edition, revised and enlarged. 8vo. Cloth, $2.

"It conveys an amount of information in the same space to be found nowhere else, and given with a clearness which renders it useful as well to the general as the professional inquirer."—*N. Y. Evening Post.*

"This volume is a standard treatise upon the subject to which it is devoted. It abounds in valuable information upon all the points bearing upon Naval Gunnery."—*N. Y. Commercial Advertiser.*

"The work is an exceedingly valuable one, and is opportunely issued."—*Boston Journal.*

D. Van Nostrand's Publications.

Totten's Naval Text-Book.

Naval Text-Book and Dictionary, compiled for the use of the Midshipmen of the U. S. Navy. By Commander B. J. TOTTEN, U. S. N. Second and revised edition. 1 vol. 12mo. $2.50.

"This work is prepared for the Midshipmen of the United States Navy. It is a complete manual of instructions as to the duties which pertain to their office, and appears to have been prepared with great care, avoiding errors and inaccuracies which had crept into a former edition of the work, and embracing valuable additional matter. It is a book which should be in the hands of every midshipman, and officers of high rank in the navy would often find it a useful companion."—*Boston Journal.*

Gunnery Inftructions.

Simplified for the Volunteer Officers of the U. S. Navy, with hints to Executive and other Officers. By Lieut. EDWARD BARRETT, U. S. N., Instructor of Gunnery, Navy Yard, Brooklyn. 1 vol. 12mo, cloth.

"It is a thorough work, treating plainly on its subject, and contains also some valuable hints to executive officers. No officer in the volunteer navy should be without a copy."—*Boston Evening Traveller.*

"Lieutenant Barrett is the Instructor in Gunnery at the U. S. Naval Station, New York. His book, which is plain, comprehensive, and abundantly illustrated, is designed to be used by naval officers as a book of reference and advice in the performance of the duties of their respective positions, and as such it is a valuable manual."—*Providence Journal.*

"I have looked through Lieut. Barrett's book, and think it will be very valuable to the volunteer officers who are now in the naval service."—C. R. P. RODGERS, *Commanding U. S. Steam Frigate Wabash.*

A Syftem of Target Practice:

For the use of Troops when armed with the Musket, Rifle-Musket, Rifle, or Carbine. Prepared, principally from the French, by Captain HENRY HETH, 10th Infantry, U. S. A.

"WAR DEPARTMENT,
"WASHINGTON, March 1st, 1858.

"The System of Target Practice, prepared under direction of the War Department by Captain Henry Heth, 10th Infantry, having been approved, is adopted for the instruction of troops when armed with the musket, rifle-musket, rifle, or carbine.
"JOHN B. FLOYD, *Secretary of War.*"

D. Van Nostrand's Publications.

Rhymed Tactics, by "Gov."

1 vol. 18mo, paper. With portraits. 25 cents.

"It will strike the military man, familiar with the tedious routine of drill, by theory, practice, and memory, as a most unique and valuable method of strengthening the latter, with the least mental exertion. The author is a thorough soldier, and his ability as a rhymester will be conceded by any intelligent reader."—*New York Leader.*

"Our author deserves great credit for the ingenuity he has displayed in putting into verse a Manual which would at first glance seem to defy the most persistent efforts of the rhymer. The book contains a number of illustrations representing some of the more difficult positions, in the figures of which portraits of several prominent officers of the New York Volunteers may be recognized."—*New York Times.*

Benét's Military Law.

A Treatise on Military Law and the Practice of Courts-Martial, by Capt. S. V. BENÉT, Ordnance Department, U. S. A., late Assistant Professor of Ethics, Law, &c., Military Academy, West Point. 1 vol., 8vo., law sheep. $3.00.

"This book is manifestly well timed just at this particular period, and it is, without doubt, quite as happily adapted to the purpose for which it was written. It is arranged with admirable method, and written with such perspicuity and in a style so easy and graceful, as to engage the attention of every reader who may be so fortunate as to open its pages. This treatise will make a valuable addition to the library of the lawyer or the civilian; while to the military man it seems to be indispensable."—*Philadelphia Evening Journal.*

"Captain Benét presents the army with a complete compilation of the precedents and decisions of rare value which have accumulated since the creation of the office of Judge Advocate, thoroughly digested and judiciously arranged, with an index of the most minute accuracy. Military Law and Courts-Martial are treated from the composition of the latter to the Finding and Sentence, with the Revision and Execution of the same, all set forth in a clear, exhaustive style that is a cardinal excellence in every work of legal reference. That portion of the work devoted to Evidence is especially good. In fact, the whole performance entitles the author to the thanks of the entire army, not a leading officer of which should fail to supply himself at once with so serviceable a guide to the intricacies of legal military government."—*N. Y. Times.*

American Military Bridges,

With India-Rubber and Galvanized Iron Pontons and Trestle Supporters, prepared for the use of the Armies of the United States. By Brig.-Gen. GEO. W. CULLUM, Major Corps of Engineers U. S. A.; Chief of the Staff of Maj.-Gen. HALLECK; Chief Engineer of the Army of the Mississippi. Second edition, with notes and two additional chapters. 1 vol. 8vo, with plates. *In Press.*

D. Van Nostrand's Publications.

Notes on Sea-Coaſt Defence:

Consisting of Sea-Coast Fortification; the Fifteen-Inch Gun; and Casemate Embrasures. By Gen. J. G. BARNARD, Corps of Engineers, U. S. Army. 1 vol. 8vo, cloth, plates. $1 50.

"This small volume by one of the most accomplished officers in the United States service is especially valuable at this time. Concisely and thoroughly Major Barnard discusses the subjects included in this volume, and gives information that will be read with great profit by military men, and by all interested in the art of war as a defensive force."—*New York Commercial.*

"It is no light compliment when we say that Major Barnard's book does no discredit to the corps to which he belongs. He writes concisely, and with a thorough knowledge of his subject."—*Russell's Army and Navy Gazette.*

A Treatiſe on the Camp and March.

With which is connected the Construction of Field Works and Military Bridges; with an Appendix of Artillery Ranges, &c. For the use of Volunteers and Militia in the United States. By Captain HENRY D. GRAFTON, U. S. A. 1 vol. 12mo, cloth. 75 cents.

Steam for the Million.

A Popular Treatise on Steam and its Application to the Useful Arts, especially to Navigation. By J. H. WARD, Commander U. S. Navy. New and revised edition. 1 vol. 8vo, cloth. $1.

"A most excellent work for the young engineer and general reader. Many facts relating to the management of the boiler and engine are set forth with a simplicity of language, and perfection of detail, that brings the subject home to the reader. Mr. Ward is also peculiarly happy in his illustrations."—*American Engineer.*

Screw Propulſion.

Notes on Screw Propulsion, its Rise and History. By Capt. W. H. WALKER, U. S. Navy. 1 vol. 8vo., cloth. 75 cents.

"Some interesting notes on screw propulsion, its rise and progress, have just been issued by Commander W. H. WALKER, U. S. N., from which all that is likely to be desired on the subject may be readily acquired. * * * After thoroughly demonstrating the efficiency of the screw, Mr. Walker proceeds to point out the various other points to be attended to in order to secure an efficient man-of-war, and eulogizes throughout the readiness of the British Admiralty to test every novelty calculated to give satisfactory results. * * * Commander Walker's book contains an immense amount of concise practical data, and every item of information recorded fully proves that the various points bearing upon it have been well considered previously to expressing an opinion."—*London Mining Journal.*

"Every engineer should have it in his library."—*American Engineer.*

www.ingramcontent.com/pod-product-compliance
Lightning Source LLC
Chambersburg PA
CBHW030305170426
43202CB00009B/880